THE REPUBLIC OF AUSTRIA
1918—1934

The Royal Institute of International Affairs is an unofficial and non-political body, founded in 1920 to encourage and facilitate the scientific study of international questions.

The Institute, as such, is precluded by its Royal Charter from expressing an opinion on any aspect of international affairs. Opinions expressed in this book are, therefore, purely individual.

THE REPUBLIC OF AUSTRIA

1918—1934

A STUDY IN THE FAILURE OF DEMOCRATIC GOVERNMENT

MARY MACDONALD

Issued under the auspices of the
Royal Institute of International Affairs

GEOFFREY CUMBERLEGE
OXFORD UNIVERSITY PRESS
LONDON NEW YORK TORONTO
1946

OXFORD UNIVERSITY PRESS
AMEN HOUSE, E.C.4
London Edinburgh Glasgow New York
Toronto Melbourne Cape Town Bombay
Calcutta Madras
GEOFFREY CUMBERLEGE
PUBLISHER TO THE UNIVERSITY

PRINTED IN GREAT BRITAIN
145 · 6393

CONTENTS

CONTENTS

INTRODUCTION

IN the autumn of 1918 the Empire of the Habsburgs collapsed; and when the Czechs, the Poles, the Southern Slavs, and the Hungarians had broken away and formed independent States, the German Provinces of the old Reich, containing some seven million out of the fifty million of the Habsburg peoples, were left alone to face an uncertain future.

The Christian Socialists of the Provinces[1] and the Social Democrats of Vienna and the industrial districts, differing in almost every other respect, were united at that time in their desire to join the German Reich, and in their intention of instituting some form of democratic government.

Frustrated by the Allies in their first objective they proceeded, with the blessing of the civilized world, to draw up with meticulous care a pronouncedly democratic constitution, which should ensure for all time government of the people, for the people, by the people. From the Cardinal Archbishop to the editor of the *Arbeiter Zeitung* there was scarcely a dissentient voice. All were agreed that from henceforward the people themselves must be the arbiters of their own fate.

The friends and enemies of Austria were equally unanimous in their approval of parliamentary democracy as a form of government. The Czechs, the Yugoslavs, and the Hungarians, in so far as they had time for consideration of Austrian affairs at all, were profoundly thankful to see the disappearance of the last remains of the old authoritarian structure of the State, for, with this destroyed, the dreaded return of the Habsburg must remain a remote contingency.

The Allies, and especially President Wilson, viewed with gratified approval the ideological change of heart evinced by their late foes. The war had been fought and won in the name of democracy, and it was consoling to see that even the ex-enemy States had come to appreciate the ideals for which so many millions of lives had been sacrificed.

[1] Throughout this study the term 'Land' will be translated as 'Province'. In fact, however, the Austrian *Ländern* were rather more important units than the term 'province' would indicate.

Finally, the Germans of the Reich, the closest friends, if not blood-brothers, of the Austrians, were themselves no less determined that they too would henceforward live under a democratic form of government.

Yet in spite of this apparently auspicious beginning, Austrian politics since 1927, and perhaps even before this, moved steadily in an anti-democratic direction. By 1929 the tide had finally turned, and at last, in February 1934, democracy in Austria was overthrown.

It is not easy to assign its just significance to each of the contributory causes of this *volte-face*, for they were many and various. The following study can only be regarded as a preliminary attempt to consider some of the most important. It can make no pretence to being an exhaustive treatment of what is a very large and complex question.

I

THE POLITICAL BACKGROUND

THE Republic of Austria was, from the first, hampered by the lack of an Austrian national consciousness strong enough to infuse any organic unity into the life of its separate Provinces. This lack, which, more than any other single cause, was to prove the ultimate undoing of the Austrian Republic, lay deeply rooted in the Habsburg past. The Germans of Austria had not been impelled by adversity to develop that patriotism which had become so marked a characteristic of the Magyar race, and which was beginning to inspire, in varying degrees, the other peoples of the Empire. German-Austrian loyalty had been concentrated upon the Habsburgs, whose policy had been supranational. German Austrians had never formed a united national group. This was partly because class divisions were felt more acutely in German circles than among the Slav peoples. But apart from this, the centrifugal tendencies existing among them had been growing, if anything, more pronounced, in the decade before the war. Some groups were purely loyalist, while others were permeated in varying degrees with pan-Germanism. There was no unifying principle at work to draw them together.

While the Habsburg experiment in a supranational empire had continued, the German Austrians had found their rich reward, for it was through the medium of the German language and culture that the Habsburgs had exercised their heterogeneous rule.[1] With the break-up of the Empire, however, the German-Austrian administrators of the Habsburgs were left high and dry; and when the centripetal influence of the Imperial House was removed, the balance of power passed from the central Government to the Provinces. 'Austria' was a meaningless concept. It was Tyrol, Salzburg, Vorarlberg,

[1] In the decades before the war, however, this practice of employing Germans as officials had been ever less rigidly adhered to, for the increasing national consciousness of the minority peoples in the Austrian half of the monarchy made essential the introduction of a certain proportion of officials conversant with the local languages, etc.

etc., which profited by a great accretion of loyalty when the Habsburgs fell.

The psychological trend towards separatism was given further impetus by economic circumstances. Vienna and the industrial parts of Lower Austria had always been accustomed to obtain their provisions from all parts of the Empire. When the more distant sources of supply were cut off, German Austria became dependent on her own resources for food. As these were quite inadequate the industrial districts could only be kept from starvation by means of a central requisitioning system, which had to be introduced as early as 1916. This was bitterly resented by the food-producing Provinces, who had scarcely enough provisions to meet their own needs.[1] The resentment was the keener because of the divergence in outlook between the Social Democrats of Vienna and the Christian Socialists of the Provinces, a factor which was to be of immense significance in the history of the Austrian Republic. This divergence was not confined to politics in the ordinary sense of the term. It embraced every sphere of activity, and affected even the minutest details of daily life. The Christian Socialist and the Social Democrat lived in two different, and for the most part antagonistic, worlds.

The net result of these centrifugal tendencies was that provincial sentiment, always a latent force behind Habsburg patriotism, increased greatly in intensity during the last months of the war. And it became obvious that, if Austria was to exist at all as an independent State, the form of her constitution must be pronouncedly federal.

All parties were agreed that the constitution must be democratic in form. This general desire for democracy was partly occasioned by war-weariness. The peoples of the Empire wanted peace at any price. Their hearts had perhaps never been wholly in the war,[2] and, as economic distress increased,

[1] In May 1918, for instance, Dr. von Seidler was forced to agree that, for purposes of food supply, North Tyrol should be joined to Bavaria, and the German districts of Northern Bohemia to Saxony. (*The Times*, 6 May 1918.)

[2] Oscar Jászi, *The Dissolution of the Habsburg Monarchy* (University of Chicago Press, 1929), pp. 14–23. Also, Edmund von Glaise-Horstenau, *Die Katastrophe* (Wien, 1929).

the discontent of the people with a government over which they could exercise virtually no control, increased with it. It came to be widely felt that an ambitious imperialistic foreign policy was responsible for the plight of the people. Men were, therefore, increasingly susceptible to the propaganda of the Allies, which was concentrated, particularly after the collapse of their Czarist ally, in representing the war as a conflict between the semi-feudal militaristic monarchies and the free democracies of the West. It was thought, also, that the Allies would be more ready to negotiate a comparatively favourable peace with Austria-Hungary if she repudiated the old autocratic régime. Moreover, Wilson's doctrine of self-determination, to which Austria with the other peoples of the Empire subscribed, necessitated a democratic state organization. Another reason for the strength of the democratic idea in German Austria was the growth in power and prestige of the Social Democratic party. There were various reasons for this. One was the stimulus of the ideas of the Russian revolution. Another was the fact that the unity, and therefore the strength, of the party was enhanced when, after the break-up of the Empire, questions of nationality ceased to divide it. Again, economic distress had embittered the working classes, who were therefore more disposed to listen to socialist teaching. And the number of workers had greatly increased as a result of the swollen war industries. At the same time inflation had undermined the economic position and power of the middle classes. Finally, the Austrian war organization, unsuccessful though it had proved to be, had accustomed people to a form of state socialism.[1]

The first years in the life of the new Republic were not happy ones. Terrible economic distress fostered the growth of extremist elements on both sides, thus serving to accentuate sharply the already existing class and party differences. The absolute dependence of Austria on economic assistance from the Allies necessitated the adoption of a foreign policy which the majority of Austrians disliked; and the control acquired

[1] Redlich, J., *Austrian War Government* (Yale University Press, 1929), pp. 123–36.

over the country by her creditors gave birth to the suspicion that government by the people for the people was synonymous with government by the Allies for the Allies.

The first election was held on 16 February 1919, one member of the National Assembly representing every 48,000 electors. 156 members were returned to the new Assembly, of whom 69 were Social Democrats, 63 Christian Socialists, 18 Pan-Germans, and 6 members of the *Landbund*. The first Republican cabinet consisted of 6 Social Democrats, headed by Chancellor Renner (who represented Austria at the Peace Conference), 5 Christian Socialists, and 4 non-party members. By the autumn of 1920, the political trend in Germany was markedly to the right, and Austria, now acutely sensitive to the German political situation, moved to the right also, exchanging a predominantly Social Democratic government for a Christian Socialist one.

The first Christian Socialist Mayr cabinet took office on 10 November 1920, and on 15 December Austria became a member of the League of Nations. But Mayr's League policy was gravely hampered by the continuance of *Anschluss* agitations, which he was unable to prevent. The weakness of his government was particularly unfortunate as the economic condition of the country was deteriorating rapidly and, as the temporary boom was over, unemployment was increasing by leaps and bounds. Strong measures were required. Mayr resigned on 1 June 1921, on the grounds that the *Anschluss* agitations had made his position impossible.

Schober succeeded him on 21 June, at the head of a cabinet comprising for the most part officials without pronounced party views.

The economic condition of the country now took a plunge downwards. The krone, which in July had stood at 110,000 to the pound, stood at 336,000 by August. The cost of living rose in two months by 124 per cent. Unemployment increased from 30,000 to 90,000, and, as the mark had by this time followed the krone, the German market was now lost.

Faced with this alarming situation Schober acted with resource and considerable courage. His ultimate aim was the launching of a loan by the Allies. But he realized that this was not likely to be forthcoming until Austria gave evidence of intending to help herself towards economic stability by every means at her disposal. *Anschluss* agitations proclaiming the impossibility of maintaining an independent State at all, and the refusal of the Social Democrats to agree to a policy of economy, the lurid stories of a starving Austria painted by international charitable societies in an endeavour to obtain funds to help her, and, finally, the huge loan proposed by Sir William Goode in 1920 as being the *sine qua non* of the rehabilitation of Austrian finances, frightened potentially friendly Governments who might in other circumstances have proffered help.

Schober and his Finance Minister, Gürtler, therefore embarked on the unpopular policy of self-help.

The Chancellor succeeded in negotiating a loan from Czechoslovakia, thus increasing his prestige in Paris and London. The pan-Germans, however, regarded the opening-up of normal and friendly relations with Czechoslovakia as sufficient reason for withdrawing their support from the Schober Government, although there was no longer any hope of reclaiming the Germans of Bohemia.

At home, Schober introduced bills reducing subsidies and increasing taxation, thus incurring the hostility of both Social Democrats and Christian Socialists. His inability to pass these measures, and to use credits to improve the condition of the country, led to his resignation on 24 May 1922. It also led to the growth of the conviction in Allied circles that it would be useless to attempt to assist Austria unless a rigid system of financial control was imposed on her.

On 24 May 1922 the Christian Socialist leader, Monsignor Seipel, formed a government. After a fruitless attempt to introduce a scheme of reform, he adopted a new policy. He sent a note to the London Conference saying that if the Allies would not help Austria they must take over its administration themselves. But as the Allies refused to be blackmailed, Seipel set off, on 20 August, on a tour.

After visiting Berlin and Prague he went to Verona where

he met the Italian Minister, Schantzer. To him he proposed that, in return for assistance, Austria should be reduced to what would virtually be an Italian protectorate. Schantzer hesitated. In the meantime a storm of expostulation arose. In view of the *rapprochement* between Italy and Hungary, France considered that the absorption of a third state into the Italian sphere of influence would constitute a grave danger to the *status quo*.

Yugoslavia and Czechoslovakia also feared for their safety, if separated by a solid block of territory under Italian influence. As a result of all this, the Convention of Geneva was signed on 4 October.

The first of the three protocols there negotiated guaranteed the political and economic independence of Austria, and her territorial integrity. By the second protocol Great Britain, France, Czechoslovakia, and Italy undertook to make Austria a loan of fifty million crowns. In the third protocol Austria agreed to put through a programme of financial reforms, and to accept control by a Commissioner-General appointed by the League.

Seipel was much criticized by the German Nationalists and the Social Democrats for submitting to foreign supervision. The latter believed that the situation could have been met by the imposition of a capital levy and that, as it was, the poorer classes would have to bear the brunt of the reforms. However, on 24 October the Protocol was accepted, and on 28 October a Reconstruction Law was passed. On 18 November inflation stopped.

Criticism of Seipel by the German Nationalists became less vociferous as time went on, for the German mark was falling rapidly, and Germany was groaning under the burden of reparations and the French invasion of the Ruhr. And opposition from the Social Democrats was to some extent silenced by the advent of Mussolini to power in Italy on 29 October.

When Seipel resigned on 12 November 1924 considerable progress had been made towards financial and economic stability, though Dr. Zimmermann, the League Commissioner, still complained of extravagance in certain directions, as for instance, the number of State employees still kept on.

The Seipel Government had been, however, handicapped by opposition from the Provinces as well as from the Viennese Social Democrats. Partly as a consequence of this experience Seipel himself became increasingly centralist in outlook. And it was no doubt in some measure owing to his influence that the constitutional reforms of 1925 were centralist in character.[1]

Although in July 1925 the Layton Rist report had struck a more hopeful note as far as the economic position of the country went, internal unrest was undoubtedly increasing steadily. *Anschluss* agitations, temporarily abandoned because of bad economic conditions in Germany, began again. The members of the Ramek Cabinet, which held office from November 1924 until October 1925, were divided in their views on this question. In any case the Cabinet could not, of course, have given the movement official support, whatever its views, as most countries made the cessation of *Anschluss* agitations the *sine qua non* of trade agreements.

On 26 October 1926 Seipel again became Chancellor, and continued as head of the Government until April 1929. It was during this period that the turning-point in Austrian politics came.

During Seipel's first term of office Vaugoin, his Minister for War, had reorganized the regular army and purged it to a large extent of its socialist proclivities. In consequence of this the *Republikanische Schutzbund* had been founded on 12 April 1923, as the party guard of the Social Democrats, who felt that their position was likely to be threatened by the advancing forces of reaction. The Christian Socialists did not, at that time, make any special efforts to form a rival organization, feeling, no doubt, that their interests were well represented in the regular army by Vaugoin. Their attitude towards the Social Democrats hardened, however, after the rioting in Vienna in July 1927.

The immediate cause of the riots was the publication of the

[1] Kelsen, *Jahrbuch des öffentlichen Rechts*, vol. xv (1927), pp. 51–101.

verdict in the Schattendorf murder trial.[1] The situation which arose was aggravated by unforeseen circumstances. For one thing, the Social Democrats did not, on this occasion, organize an orderly demonstration as was their custom. The workers, therefore, left the factories on their own initiative, and surged in disorganized groups into the centre of the city, where they eventually succeeded in setting fire to the Justiz Palast. The police appear to have lost their heads and fired on onlookers as well as rioters, causing unnecessary loss of life, and thereby inflaming the passions of the demonstrators to such an extent that their own leaders could not control them.

This incident greatly embittered the working classes, who professed themselves appalled at the callousness shown by the Government in quelling the riots. On the other hand, Christian Socialist circles thought they saw in the rioting the incipient danger of Bolshevism, and became, in consequence, very much more disposed to support the *Heimwehr* and similar semi-fascist organizations.

The antagonism between Monsignor Seipel on the one hand, and the Social Democrat leaders on the other, became more bitter than ever before as, rightly or wrongly, the Social Democrats believed that Seipel had been mainly responsible for what they considered to be the unnecessarily brutal methods employed in putting down the riots.[2] They therefore gave positive encouragement to their supporters to leave the Church, knowing that this would be by far the most effective weapon against Seipel.

It was after the July rioting of 1927 that the *Heimwehr* movement first began to play an important part in Austrian politics.

[1] In the previous January several persons had been shot by *Heimwehr* men in the course of a clash between *Heimwehr* and Social Democrat demonstrators at Schattendorf, a small village in the Burgenland. The case was a complicated one, and it was found to be very difficult to assess the blame fairly between the two contending parties. The *Heimwehr* men concerned were eventually acquitted. This confirmed the Viennese Social Democrats in the belief which, rightly or wrongly, was coming to be widely held, that it was impossible for Social Democrats to get a fair hearing in the courts.

[2] Seipel unfortunately remarked afterwards, when the ringleaders were on trial, that no mercy should be shown them. This expression, '*Keine Milde*', was always remembered against him.

This organization had sprung up in the immediate post-war period, as a self-help movement among the peasantry in several of the Provinces, notably in Carinthia.[1] The various groups were generally led by the local nobility, lawyers, and school-teachers of the villages and the small country towns. These groups had no definite aims beyond the general intention of protecting peasant and other property against the depredations of the Yugoslavs and the 'Reds'.

It is probable that the movement would have lapsed once law and order was established, had it not been fostered by Seipel and right-wing Christian Socialist groups. As it was, the *Heimwehr*, after 1927, went from strength to strength, until it finally disintegrated before the rising tide of the Nazis in 1932.

The seeds of discord were present in it from the first. On the one hand there were the remnants of the pre-war German Nationalists, the intelligentsia of the country towns and villages, the school-teachers, shopkeepers, and small industrialists; on the other hand there were the old ruling classes, who were largely backed by the higher clergy (Prince Starhemberg is reported to have described the *Heimwehr* as "un movement religieux pour la protection non seulement de la patrie, mais aussi de la foi catholique traditionelle et de la culture chrétienne contre les ravages du libéralisme"), the big industrialists, and, later, by the Italians. The former group became ever more Nazi in outlook, as the Nazi movement grew in Germany. The other and smaller groups were not Nazi but monarchist in sympathy. However, before 1930 none of the groups in the *Heimwehr* movement was exclusive in personnel or aims.

It may be said that by 1927, when the *Heimwehr* began to arm its members on a large scale, both wings had ceased to be in any way representative of the peasants. Indeed, there seems reason to believe that the majority of the peasants, much as they disliked 'Red Vienna', viewed the fascist proclivities

[1] C. A. Macartney, 'The Armed Formations of Austria', *Journal of the Institute of International Affairs*, vol. viii, 1929. Also Dr. Kurt von Schuschnigg, *Farewell, Austria* (Cassell, 1938), pp. 113–29.

of the *Heimwehr* leaders with even greater misgiving.[1] It was said that peasants who took part in *Heimwehr* demonstrations were frequently forced to do so against their will.[2]

In the years following 1927 there was an ever-increasing number of incidents between Social Democrats and *Heimwehr* demonstrators. Indeed, whenever the two groups arranged demonstrations, fighting broke out. And other groups on the Christian Socialist side, anxious to have their interests represented in what everybody came to feel would be the inevitable armed struggle for power, began forming their own paramilitary bodies.[3]

It must in justice be remarked that the party leaders of the Social Democrats appear to have been very much more acutely conscious of the danger inherent in these developments than were their rivals. They made repeated efforts in the years after 1927 to persuade the Christian Socialists to agree to disarm. Christian Socialist counter-proposals were, however, always coupled with demands which the Social Democrats felt they could not accept, such as cessation of opposition in Parlia-

[1] Groups in the Bauernbund, one of the largest of the peasant organizations, became increasingly critical of *Heimwehr* aims and methods: see article of Schumy, their Vice-president, in *Neues Wiener Tageblatt*, 'Man kann nicht Demokrat sein u. gleichzeitig den Parlamentarismus glatt verwerfen', etc. (quoted in the *Frankfurter Zeitung* of 26 August 1929). 'Solange die Heimwehrbewegung ihre Hauptstütze im Bauerntum hatte u. die Vertreter der Bauernschaft ihr Wort entscheidend in die Wagschale werfen konnten, war auch nie von einem Angriff, von einem Marsch nach Wien, die Rede. Diese Zieländerungen sind erst zu tage getreten als sich der Einfluss der ehemaligen Aristokraten, Generäle u. Stabsoffiziere in der Heimwehr über Gebuhr erhob. Nun waren aber gerade diese Herren nicht fähig uns in eine neue bessere Zeit zu führen; denn wir können uns nicht erninnern dass sie sich in den Tagen ihrer Macht unserer besonders angenommen hätten.' (Article in the *Bauern Zeitung*, the organ of *Bauernbund* in Upper Austria, quoted in the *Frankfurter Zeitung* of 25 August 1929.)

[2] 'Demonstrations' is perhaps a misleading term. Both the *Heimwehr* and the *Republikanische Schutzbund* were accustomed to use rifles, bayonets, hand-grenades, tear-gas bombs, and similar weapons. The *Heimwehr* had machine-guns and batteries of artillery. They were organized as a fighting force, and it was their custom to establish base hospitals, field-kitchens, etc., when they held their 'demonstrations'. (See the account in the *Manchester Guardian* of 8 October 1928, of the big Wiener Neustadt demonstration.)

[3] For instance, the *Sturmscharen* of Schuschnigg, a militant Catholic youth body, and the *Freiheitsbund* of Kunschak, a left-wing Christian Socialist working-class organization.

ment.[1] The intransigence of the right-wing parties was probably due to the fact that they were well aware that they were in reality very much stronger than their rivals, and would almost certainly win if it came to a trial of strength.

The internal situation in Austria grew ever more chaotic in the years 1929–34. Obstruction by the Social Democrats, and the growing impatience of the *Heimwehr* and the right-wing groups with the forms of democratic government, made the working of any kind of parliamentary system increasingly difficult.[2]

The position further deteriorated in the autumn of 1930, for the November elections revealed, for the first time, a split in the ranks of the once united bourgeois front. Schober then organized a National Economic Bloc, consisting of the German Nationalists, the moderate Christian Socialists, and the *Landbund*.[3] Seipel and the clericals, with the Vienna and Lower Austrian *Heimwehr* under Major Fey, together formed an anti-Marxist front.

This split in the bourgeois ranks was viewed with favour by the moderate groups, who were glad to cut loose the extremist elements. But in fact it heralded the beginning of the end, for it meant that, in future, right-wing Governments had to be formed by uncertain coalitions, and were therefore tempted to look for support to extra-parliamentary bodies.

The comparative quiet of 1931 proved to be the lull before the storm. The *Heimwehr* movement was greatly weakened by quarrels among its leaders, and, as *Heimwehr* roots among the peasantry were shallow, little was heard of it. Attention was,

[1] An important, though numerically small, section of the Christian Socialists, led by Kunschak, continued, however, to work for conciliation with the Social Democrats. In the pages of their paper, the *Weltblatt*, they pointed out, over and over again, the dangers of intransigence. But Kunschak fought a losing battle against the extremists of his party, and in May 1929 he resigned from its vice-chairmanship, a post which he had long held, after defeat on his conciliation policy.

[2] On 18 May 1930, the *Heimwehr* leaders published the famous Korneuberger Programme, by which they pledged themselves to make an end of parliamentary democracy and the party system, and to institute a form of fascist government, using force if necessary to achieve their aims.

[3] With the exception of the branches in Salzburg and Upper Austria. These remained independent.

moreover, diverted to the project of the Customs Union with Germany, in the first months of the year.

In 1932 the storm broke, and the Nazi party emerged for the first time as a strong force in Austrian politics. The *Landbund* and the old German Nationalist party were quickly swallowed up. The *Heimwehr* movement split in two, the members of the larger group becoming openly or covertly partisans of the Nazis. The peasants and the members of the moderate wing of the Christian Socialists turned in despair to Dr. Dolfuss as the one man who might save them.

Dr. Dolfuss did succeed in evoking, for the first time, the faint beginnings of an Austrian national consciousness. But his Government was too weak to withstand simultaneous attacks from the left and from the right. After having dissolved a parliament which had become unworkable in March 1933, he found himself confronted with the necessity of coming to terms either with the Social Democrats or with the *Heimwehr*, now powerfully supported by Italy. He chose the latter course. The direct result was the crushing of the Social Democrats in February 1934, and the end of the Austrian experiment in democratic government.

II

PRELIMINARY DISCUSSIONS ON THE FORM OF THE NEW CONSTITUTION

THE break-up of the Empire necessitated a radical alteration of the pre-war Austrian constitution, the pivot of which had been the Imperial House. The chief object of Habsburg policy had been to manipulate the rival national and social forces within the State in order to ensure the predominance of Imperial influence. Therefore, with the collapse of the Monarchy and the falling away of the non-German elements, German Austria was confronted with the task of building up a new national State, which was necessarily different, in both its forms and its aims, from that which had preceded it.

Because of the general feeling that the reintroduction of any form of autocratic government, however convenient this might be in a period of emergency, must be avoided at all costs, the governmental devices made use of by the German Austrians from October 1918 to the promulgation of the constitution of October 1920[1] were marked by a desire to safeguard the position of the National Assembly as the supreme legislative organ.[2] All parties were agreed, though their fervour varied, that the new State must be a democratic one.

The stress on the importance of the Lower House was also partly a consequence of the political philosophy of the Social Democrats, whose views were then in the ascendant. This party laid great emphasis on the necessity for concentrating power in one democratically elected Chamber, and viewed with suspicion attempts on the part of that Chamber to delegate any considerable part of its authority to bodies not directly

[1] For an analysis of the Constitutions of 30 October and 19 December 1918 and 14 March 1919, see Kelsen, '*Die Verfassung Deutschösterreichs*', *Jahrbuch des öffentlichen Rechts* (Tübingen), vol. ix, pp. 245–91.

[2] Kelsen, *Die Verfassungsgesetze der Republik Österreich* (Wien, 1919).

elected by the people.[1] The party therefore regarded with disfavour any of the customary devices designed to check the Chamber, such as a strong Government, a strong President, or a second Chamber. Social Democrats were equally anxious to vindicate the independence of the Chamber as against the people. Hence, they regarded such devices as the Referendum and the Initiative with suspicion. For this reason, also, they were in favour of the introduction of proportional representation with the closed list system, as they believed that these would free the members of the Chamber from any kind of dependence on their constituents. This, they hoped, would avert both the corruption of local politics and the predominance of the provincial outlook in the National Assembly, which they feared would result if this became the catspaw of local groups.[2]

These views can be clearly traced in the constitutional experiments of the first two years of the Republic. For instance, the Council of State was chosen by the National Assembly on the basis of proportional representation. The Government was thus recruited not from the ranks of one party, but from the whole body of representatives.[3] This body was, however, intended to be in all respects subordinate to the National Assembly. The three Presidents of the Council, who had equal powers, were chosen by each of the three big parties, the Christian Socialists, the Social Democrats, and the German Nationalists.[4] The elections to the Constituent Assembly in February 1919 were based on proportional representation, instead of the old majority voting arrangement.

[1] For instance, the Executive Committee, or Council of State elected by the National Assembly and entrusted by it, on 30 October, with the task of carrying on the government of the country, was deliberately made subordinate to the National Assembly, of which it was constituted the executive committee. The Council of State was, however, later given a right of suspensive veto on proposals put forward by the National Assembly. Law of 19 December 1918. St. G. Bl. Nr. 139, Article 4. Law of 14 March 1919, St. G. Bl. Nr. 179, Article 5.

[2] Renner, speech to Provincial National Assembly, 18 December 1918.

[3] 30 October 1918, St. G. Bl. Nr. 1, Article 4.

[4] Hauser, Seitz, and Dinghofer were elected by the Christian Socialists, the Social Democrats, and the German Nationalists respectively on 21 October 1918. Each held in rotating weeks the offices of President of the National Assembly, the Council of State, and what may be termed the Cabinet.

But, while Social Democrat ideas regarding the establishment of a strong unitary State in which power would be as far as possible concentrated in a single democratically elected Chamber, came to prevail in the capital, the situation in the Provinces was developing along quite different lines. New Provincial Assemblies, which had been set up in place of the old *Landtags*, had come to regard themselves as quasi-independent legislative bodies. And the central Government, still uncertain of itself, pursued a somewhat vacillating policy with regard to them.[1] For instance, although no provision was made for the participation of the Provinces as such in legislation in the Provisional Constitution of 30 October 1918,[2] and although on 14 November the State formally took over control in the Provinces,[3] the Executive Committee had, on 29 October, sent a mandate to all the Provincial Assemblies,[4] asking them to draw up provisional constitutions containing declarations of accession to the Republic. This mandate was really, as Kelsen remarked, the *reductio ad absurdum* of the extreme federalist view.[5] Some of the Provinces took no notice of it.[6] Others merely made declarations of accession.[7] None the less, a decree of 12 November took notice of the "solemn declarations of accession of the Provinces and districts of the State territory".[8]

[1] Kelsen, 'Die Verfassung Deutschösterreichs', *Jahrbuch des öffentlichen Rechts*, vol. ix. p. 25: 'In den Ländern glaubte man vielfach, ein von der Zentralregierung gänzlich unabhängiges Gesetzgebungsrecht zu haben, u. auch der Staatsrat schien kein eigentliches Sanktionsrecht den Landesgesetzebeschlüssen gegenüber in Anspruch nehmen zu wollen.'

[2] Staats Gesetz Blatt. Nr. 1, Article 2. 'Die gesetzgebende Gewalt wird von der provisorischen Nationalversammlung selbst ausgeübt.'

[3] St. G. Bl. Nr. 124.

[4] The position of these Assemblies was a somewhat anomalous one, for they were not, strictly speaking, democratic bodies, as they had been elected on the old Curia system. (See Austria-Hungary Handbooks prepared under the direction of the Historical Section at the Foreign Office, No. 1, pp. 9 and 11.)

[5] 'Die Länder sollten durch diese Erklärung einem Staate erst beitreten ... obgleich er schor vor dieser Beitrittserklärung bereits als constituiert angesehen werden musste. Vom Standpunkt des Verfassungsbeschlusses vom 30 October, u. des Landesgesetzes vom 14 November waren diese Beitrittserklärungen nicht bloss verfassungswidrig sondern geradezu sinnlos.' *Jahrbuch des öffentlichen Rechts*, vol. ix, p. 259.

[6] Lower Austria, Tyrol.

[7] Upper Austria, Vorarlberg.

[8] St. G. Bl. Nr. 23.

And on 14 November a law was passed providing for the election by local assemblies of a *Landeshauptmann* or Governor and subordinates, who were to take over all the business formerly transacted by the State officials and the Statthalter, appointed by the Emperor.[1] This meant, in effect, the abolition of the dual system, and a large measure of decentralization in administrative matters.[2]

The position as regards the relationship between the State and the Provinces throughout the first two years of the Republic was, therefore, somewhat obscure; and this state of affairs not unnaturally resulted in the strengthening of separatist feeling. Traces of this may be seen in the provisions drawn up regarding provincial legislation on 14 March 1919.[3] It was then laid down that laws passed by Provincial Assemblies required counter-signature by a Secretary of State or the Chancellor. But even if assent was refused the Provincial Assembly could, if it wished, then reintroduce and pass the bill. If, however, provincial legislation required the co-operation of the State for its implementation, the Government, acting as a whole, could refuse assent. The Government thus had a suspensive, but not an absolute veto over provincial legislation.

The different opinions which, as has been pointed out, prevailed in Vienna, where the Social Democrats were in power, and the Provinces, which were for the most part Christian Socialist strongholds, came to the fore strongly at the various conferences held regarding the form of the final constitution.[4]

The main demand of the Christian Socialist party, after the withdrawal of the Emperor, was that German Austria must be a federal State, in which the member States would have relatively far-reaching rights of self-government.[5] The reasons adduced by the party in support of its federalist programme

[1] St. G. Bl. Nr. 24.

[2] Eisenmann, *La Constitution Fédérale de la Republique d'Autriche* (Paris, 1924), pp. 37–8.

[3] St. G. Bl. Nr. 179.

[4] See Appendix A.

[5] The views of the more extreme federalists, such as Dr. Ender, amounted in fact to a claim that Austria should become a federation of independent States.

were various. Many of them were characterized by an appeal to the medieval past, when, it was asserted, each Province had had a virtually autonomous status.[1] The only link between them had been superimposed in course of time by the Habsburgs. When the Habsburg superstructure disappeared they reverted to their former position of independence.[2]

It was obvious, however, that the federalist policy of the Christian Socialists was inspired for the most part by more practical reasons. The party as a whole was animated by intense dislike of 'Red' Vienna, and feared that a disproportionate amount of power would fall to her, as the capital city, if a unitary State were established.

This antagonism, already in existence before the war, was sharpened by the events following on the Armistice. It was felt, for instance, that the Social Democrats, who were then in control of the Government, had made no attempt to protect the Provinces against the attacks of marauding bands of soldiers, although Vienna had had both the arms and the men necessary.[3] The secrecy of Viennese foreign policy was also mistrusted, for it was widely believed that everything was being sacrificed to the policy of *Anschluss*, a policy which the Christian Socialists regarded with increasing misgiving after the Spartacist rising of 1918 in Germany, and the subsequent Communist disturbances.[4] The economic policy of Vienna was also much disliked, and the socialization projects were strenuously resisted. Opposition in the Provinces to the requisitioning system, which had to be continued even after the Armistice, amounted at times to economic blockade.

[1] Speech by Dr. Ender at the Salzburg Provincial Conference, February 1920, *Stenographische Verhandlungschrift*, p. 28, 'Bevor Österreich-Ungarn bestanden hat, hat Tyrol bestanden, u. wird weiter bestehen'. Also, Seipel, 'Die Absonderung der Länder', *Politische Gesellschaft*, 14 May 1919, and Seipel, *Der Kampf um die österreichische Verfassung* (Wien, 1930), pp. 74–6.

[2] It was pointed out that the Provisional National Assembly had virtually recognized this fact by inviting the Provinces, on 29 October 1918, to announce their accession to the new State of German Austria. (Speech by Ehrer at the Salzburg Provincial Conference, op. cit., p. 20.)

[3] Seipel, 'Die Absonderung der Länder', *Politische Gesellschaft*, 14 May 1919, pp. 74–6.

[4] In the Draft Constitution of 12 November 1918, which was passed as a temporary measure by the National Assembly, it was stated that "German Austria is a part of the German Republic". (St. G. Bl. Nr. 5, Article 2.)

There were, however, men in the Christian Socialist party, as, for instance, the Prälat Hauser, who saw clearly the danger of allowing particularism in the Provinces to assume too great proportions, and who realized that the future well-being of the Austrian Republic must depend upon the breaking-down of existing barriers between the peasants and the workers. But, although the federalist policy of the Christian Socialists was probably to a large extent dictated by opportunist reasons, there was a certain positive substratum beneath these. As Herr Steidle remarked at the Salzburg Provincial Conference, federalism was a form of government particularly well adapted to the German mentality, with its love for complex organizations.[1]

The Christian Socialist party devoted much attention to the composition of the Upper or Federal Chamber. The more extreme federalists were of the opinion that each member State should have equal representation, on the Swiss model, irrespective of the size of its territory or the numbers of its population, on the ground that all the Provinces were equal and independent member States of the Federation. More moderate federalists were, however, prepared to envisage some kind of differential representation, which would take such differences into account.[2] In this case also, the views of the Christian Socialists were coloured by the knowledge that their position in the small Provinces like Tyrol and Vorarlberg was

[1] 'Die deutsche Nationaleigentümlichkeit war immer auf den Foderalismus aufgebaut. Das war seit undenklichen Zeiten so, das liegt den Deutchen im Blut.' (Steidle, Salzburg Provincial Conference, op. cit., p. 48.) Cf. Seipel, *Nation u. Staat* (Wien, 1916), and Mayr, '100 Sitzung der konstituierenden National Versammlung der Republik Österreich', *Stenographisches Protokoll*, p. 3383.

[2] The populations of the nine Provinces were as follows:

Province	Area (sq. miles)	Population
Vienna	107	1,863,783
Lower Austria	7,462	1,478,697
Upper Austria	4,628	873,702
Salzburg	2,763	222,731
Styria	6,327	977,350
Carinthia	3,684	370,432
Tyrol	4,790	313,699
Vorarlberg	1,005	139,968
Burgenland	1,586	286,299

a very strong one, whereas it was very much less strong in the large, semi-industrial Provinces, as Upper and Lower Austria.

As regards the position of the future President of the Republic, the Christian Socialists were of the opinion that he should be directly elected. This, they hoped, would enable him to adopt a more independent position *vis-à-vis* a possible Social Democrat majority in the Lower House. This proposal was, however, strongly contested by the Social Democrats, who feared that it would be the thin end of the wedge of authoritarian government.

The Christian Socialists wished provision to be made for the direct participation of the people in the business of government, through the Referendum and the Initiative.[1]

But, if it can be said of the Christian Socialists that their views on the new constitution were occasioned for the most part by the political exigencies of the moment rather than by abstract views on the best form of government, the same can certainly be said of the Social Democrats. Their opposition to federalism, for instance, was undoubtedly largely occasioned by fear of reactionary tendencies in the Provinces. They maintained that Christian Socialist contentions regarding the historic individuality of the Provinces were illusory. Most of the Provinces, they argued, had simply grown out of the inheritances of the great feudal families, and were often quite unsuitable as economic units.[2] In any case, many of them had had their boundaries so altered in the course of the war as to make ridiculous any attempt to identify them with pre-war units. The districts which remained were often so situated as to make them quite unsuitable for maintenance even as units of common administration.[3] In any case most of the so-called rights of self-government enjoyed by the Provinces had only

[1] It is interesting to find that Seipel was a particularly strong supporter of these devices. He specially approved, for instance, of the provision that minorities in three different Provinces should be enabled to join together, if by so doing they could amass the requisite 300,000 votes for an Initiative. ('Verfassungsreform u. Wirtschaftsleben', *Reichspost*, 15 February 1920. Also, Seipel, *Der Kampf um die österreichische Verfassung*, pp. 77–9.)

[2] Resel, Salzburg Provincial Conference, op. cit., p. 22.

[3] Speech by Gruener, Salzburg Provincial Conference, op. cit., p. 16; cf. Grogger, op. cit., p. 27.

been acquired in the course of the last few months. There was now no reason for encouraging federalist sentiment since the nationality problem no longer existed and the duplication of administrative machinery would entail expenditure on a scale which the new Republic could ill afford.[1] Moreover, the National Assembly was itself only a *Landtag* of the German Reich.[2]

The Social Democrats were, however, sufficiently realist in their politics to admit that the federal principle would have to be to some extent incorporated in the new State organization. They therefore concentrated upon the mitigation of what they considered its most obvious dangers.[3]

They were strongly in favour of the introduction of the unicameral system for the legislature. In their view, if the Upper House had no power as against the Lower House, it was merely a piece of unnecessary machinery. If the Upper House had such power, and was indirectly elected, the democratic body would be made responsible to an only indirectly democratic body. If, on the other hand, the Upper House were directly elected, it would in all probability be merely a replica of the Lower House.[4] However, the party as a whole realized that the introduction of the unicameral system was not practical politics. They therefore concentrated on an attempt to eliminate, as far as possible, the federal character of the Upper House. It must be elected, they maintained, on a population basis, as it would obviously be

[1] Dolser, Salzburg Provincial Conference, op. cit., p. 50; cf. Preussler, 4th Sitzung, 14 March 1919.

[2] The Social Democrats feared that the development of a federal system would make the conclusion of an *Anschluss* with Germany more difficult, since Germany would not be prepared to recognize this arrangement.

[3] Herr Danneberg, for instance, in the debate on the final proposals laid before the Constituent National Assembly, urged that, since a federal constitution was to be adopted, the existing boundaries of the Provinces should not be considered as in any way sacrosanct, and that, in order to safeguard the democratic principle, it should be provided that, if a part of a Province having a population equal to or greater than that of Vorarlberg, wished to join another Province, or form an independent Province, they should, as provided in the new German Constitution, be permitted to do so. (100 Sitzung, Constituent National Assembly, p. 3386.)

[4] Speech by Grüber, Salzburg Provincial Conference, op. cit., p. 65.

undemocratic to give equal representation to Provinces whose population figures were so unequal. The party also aimed at curtailing its power as far as possible.

The Social Democrats disliked the Christian Socialist project of a President directly elected by the people. They thought it better that the functions of a President should be discharged by the President of the National Council. Direct election of a President would, they feared, inevitably introduce an autocratic element into the Government.[1]

They were somewhat lukewarm in their support of direct legislation by the people through the Initiative and the Referendum, as these devices would tend, they thought, to undermine the omnipotence of the National Assembly. A dangerous element of procrastination would be introduced into the business of government and misunderstandings would inevitably occur as it was almost always impossible to answer 'yes' or 'no' to complicated legislative projects. It would be much better to let the people exercise their control by shortening the legislative period.[2]

The Social Democrats were emphatically of the opinion that the democratization of government and administration in the Provinces was the *sine qua non* of democratic progress, particularly if a federal system was to be introduced.[3]

The views of the German Nationalists need not be considered in detail, for they did not materially influence the drafting of the constitution. It may be noted, however, that they, like the Christian Socialists, showed a tendency to distrust the autocracy of the Lower House. For this reason, they were anxious to secure direct election for the President.[4] And they were prepared to envisage an even wider use of the Initiative and

[1] Speech by Danneberg, Stenographische Verhandlungschrift über die Länderkonferenz in Linz, 1920, pp. 22–3; and 100 Sitzung, Constituent National Assembly, p. 3390. It is interesting to note that Kelsen, one of the authors of the 1920 Constitution, was also strongly of the opinion that the direct election of the President would mean, in reality, a weakening rather than a strengthening of the democratic principle. (*Jahrbuch des öffentlichen Rechts*, 1920, vol. ix, op. cit., p. 281.)

[2] Danneberg, 100 Sitzung, Constituent National Assembly, p. 3396.

[3] Grüber, Linz Provincial Conference, op. cit., p. 9.

[4] 100 Sitzung, Constituent National Assembly, p. 3400.

the Referendum than were most of the Christian Socialists.[1] Some of the Social Democrats were anxious for the establishment of an Economic Chamber which would have at least large advisory powers, side by side with the National Council and the Federal Council. In this Chamber, employers and employees should be equally represented.[2] The Social Democrats, however, wanted above all things, union with Germany.

[1] Langoth, *Stenographische Verhandlungschrift über die Länderkonferenz* in Linz Provincial Conference, April 1920, p. 11.
[2] Ibid., p. 12.

III

THE CONSTITUTION OF 1920

THE constitution, which was finally promulgated on 5 October 1920, represented in the main a compromise between the views of the Christian Socialists and the Social Democrats.

(i) *The Democratic Principle*

All parties were agreed that the new constitution must be a democratic one. It was therefore laid down in the first Article that "Austria is a democratic Republic. Her laws are made by the people."[1] A great effort was made to secure effectively, by careful legislation, the democratization of the whole machinery of government. It is only necessary, for instance, to refer to the detailed provisions made by Articles 95 and 115–20 to ensure the democratization of the machinery of government in the Provinces. In the case of these Articles, zeal for the triumph of the democratic principle overcame objections to provisions which constituted a striking encroachment on provincial rights.

Again, the importance attached by the framers of the constitution to the firm establishment of the democratic principle is shown by the provisions dealing with the organization of the

[1] Dr. Kelsen points out that this statement is without much legal significance. 'Ob Österreich eine demokratische Republik sei oder nicht, das zu beurteilen ist auschliesslich u. allein Sache der Rechtserkenntnis, nicht des Rechtes; dessen Sache ist es eine demokratische Republik zu sein oder nicht zu sein.' And the second part of the article is misleading in so far as it implies that direct government by the people is the normal method of legislative procedure. Actually, direct government can only be used under exceptional circumstances (vide Articles 41–6 of the Constitution). (*Juhrbuch des öffentlichen Rechts*, 1922, vol. xi, p. 238.) These statements may be compared with, for instance, the first clause of Article 87, 'Die Richter sind in Ausübung ihres richterlichen Amtes unabhängig', and with the first clause of Article 91, 'Das Volk hat an der Rechtsprechung mitzuwirken', neither of which statements has in itself any legal significance.

suffrage. In 1907 the suffrage had been extended for State elections so that all males over twenty-four years of age had an active vote, and all males over twenty-nine had a passive one. These age limits were now reduced to twenty and twenty-four years respectively; and the right to vote was extended to women.

Whereas in pre-war days no attempt had been made to regulate the suffrage in those Provinces where the old curial system, abolished for Reichstag elections in 1907, had persisted up to the war, it was now expressly laid down that the right to vote in provincial elections might never be more restricted than it was for elections to the National Council.[1] This provision is another example of a striking incursion on provincial rights in the interests of democracy.

By Article 26, (5), it was laid down that the right to elect to the National Council could only be suspended by judicial decree,[2] and that it was intended that this right should only be withdrawn for reasons of the utmost gravity is suggested by Article 142, (3), which decrees that even in the case of an adverse judgement by the Constitutional Court in a case of impeachment of an official, a temporary loss of political rights should only follow if the case were one of particularly grave circumstances. And by Article 149, (2), Article 20 of the Fundamental Law of 21 December 1867 and the Law of 5 May 1869, dealing with temporary suspension of these rights, were both expressly repealed.

It was felt, however, that the establishment and safeguarding of universal suffrage was not in itself sufficient to ensure the triumph of the democratic principle. Before the war, for instance, although a comparatively wide, direct and secret suffrage had been in force, the equality of the suffrage had

[1] Vide Article 95, (2).

[2] By this Article, the arrangement by which women under the surveillance of the police were deprived of the right to vote (Law of 18 December 1918, 139) was abrogated. Verdier suggests that Dr. Kelsen felt that no one should be subjected to the loss of so fundamental a right, 'par une simple décision administrative qui risque souvent, et en particulier lorsqu'elle est prise par la police, d'être arbitraire'. (Verdier, *La Constitution fédérale de la Republique d'Autriche*, Paris, 1924, p. 115.)

been to a large extent illusory, because of the inequality in apportionment of mandates to the constituencies, which differed greatly in size. The introduction of proportional representation had to some extent removed these inequalities. And by a Law of 18 December 1918 mandates were redistributed over the constituencies. The new allocation was calculated on the basis of the census published in 1910. But Verdier points out that the constituencies still received mandates only in rough approximation to the number of their inhabitants.[1] And Kelsen himself admits that the weight of the individual vote varied not a little in the different constituencies.[2] However, it was considered useless to reapportion mandates until the boundaries of the State had been finally settled by the Treaty of St. Germain.[3] Meantime, the inequality of the existing arrangement had been increased by subsequent movements of population. However, by Article 26, (2), of the 1920 constitution, the principle of the apportionment of mandates to the constituencies on a basis strictly proportional to their populations was established. And the Electoral Law of 11 July 1923 laid down the method to be used for ascertaining the correct apportionment.[4]

It was felt by many, however, that the division of the electorate into constituencies in itself constituted a violation of the democratic principle, in that such a division resulted in a curtailment of the freedom of members, who then tended to act as the delegates of their constituents rather than as free representatives of the whole people. Renner, in particular, emphasized the dangers of this system. He feared that the politics of the State might come to turn upon local issues, while what should have been the essential questions, the different views of the various parties, would fade into the

[1] Verdier calculates that in Salzburg 18,116 persons were represented by one deputy, while in south-west Vienna 28,332 persons had only one deputy (ibid., p. 116).

[2] *Die Verfassungsgesetze der Republik Österreich*, vol. ii, p. 7.

[3] Verdier, op. cit., pp. 116–17

[4] It is probable that the inequalities of the previous system were somewhat exaggerated, as when fresh elections were held on 21 October 1923, in accordance with the new census of March and the Electoral Law of July, only slight alterations were found to be necessary.

background.[1] He further pointed out that such a state of affairs would tend to produce a deadlock in the National Council, for as members would be bound by the local views of their constituents, they would be unable to negotiate the necessary compromises with their colleagues. Moreover, the candidate prepared to offer the most bribes to his constituents was likely to be elected.[2]

It is clearly undeniable that the division of a country into constituencies must, in so far as it has any political consequence at all, tend to tip the balance of a constitution in favour of direct democracy, by encouraging control of particular members by particular territorial groups. It is, therefore, not surprising that the constituency system met with opposition, particularly from the Social Democrats, for the tendency of left-wing political theorists at that time was to revert to the nineteenth-century idea of the omnipotence of Parliament and its freedom from the electorate once it had been elected.

The constitution of 1920, in this, as in so many other instances, represented a compromise. By Article 56, for instance, it was expressly laid down that members of the National Council and the Federal Council should not be bound by instructions. But the constituency system was maintained. On the other hand, the closed list system was introduced, thus lessening the direct connection between members and their constituents.[3] And for the majority system there was substi-

[1] Speech by Renner in the Provisional National Assembly on the occasion of the introduction of the Electoral Law of 18 December 1918. 'Die Wahlkreiseinteilung gab der Landverteilung ein imperatives Mandat, u. stellte sie unter die Peitsche einer rücksichtslosen Agitation, die ihnen jede Freiheit der Entschliessung nahm . . . Dass wir bisher nicht jene grosse Parteiformation nach allgemeinen Weltanschauungen herausbilden konnten wie in anderen Ländern, geht zum guten Teil auf diese mechanische Spaltung der Wählerschaft zurück.' (Quoted by Kelsen, op. cit., vol. ii, p. 43.)

[2] In fact, however, Renner's fears proved to be groundless. The difficulty lay rather in the fact that the connection between electors and their representatives was so remote that the former could not exercise any control at all.

[3] In point of fact, the closed list system, in that it inevitably tended to make members dependent on their party caucuses, was just as liable to lead to a diminution in the authority of Parliament through the subordination of its members to extra-parliamentary groups, as was the constituency system.

This device was criticized as unsatisfactory by Adamovich (*Grundriss des österreichischen Staatsrechts*, Vienna, 1927, p. 136). In May 1927 a minis-

tuted a far-reaching system of proportional representation which, by its provision for combinations of minorities in the various constituencies, meant that a given proportion of members of the National Council was not responsible to particular territorial groups. It was hoped that by this means the advantages of the constituency system could be maintained without what was felt to be its disadvantage—unrepresented minorities in all the constituencies.

The Austrian constitution of 1920 was riddled with provisions for the representation of minorities. No man should, it was felt, be faced with the alternative of voting for parties with whose policy he was not in complete agreement or of wasting his vote. But in fact this attempt to obviate the necessity for compromise, which is the kernel of the theory of proportional representation, cannot solve the problem, as was shown only too clearly by the later course of events in Austria. The need for compromise in a positive State composed of divergent elements cannot be evaded. The advocates of proportional representation merely shift the responsibility for the compromise from the elector to his representative. For, in a Parliament or any other body fully representative of public opinion (which will be, as a rule, a body composed of small groups), bargaining among the parties must always be necessary before a governmental majority can be formed at all. It may well be argued that the majority system, which leaves the business of compromising to the elector himself, is the more democratic of the two methods.

However, the principle of proportional representation came to be regarded at that time by almost all Austrians as the safeguard *par excellence* for democratic government.[1] Thus,

---

terial declaration incorporated a scheme to give the voter more control over the nomination of candidates. The idea was again discussed at the time of the 1929 reforms, and was brought up whenever the question of a possible reform of Parliament arose.

[1] Speech by Renner in the Provisional National Assembly, on 18 December 1918 (Kelsen, op. cit., vol. ii, p. 45). The Austrian system may be compared with the automatic quota system of the German constitution. The German method has the advantage of simplicity. It also provides a stimulus to vote, since for every additional 60,000 votes a further mandate is allotted.

although in the Electoral Law of 18 December 1918 no provisions were made for the combination of minorities in the various constituencies—provision having been made, on the contrary, for amalgamations of parties[1]—the Law of July 1920 provided that fifteen mandates should be apportioned to those parties which had unused votes in the various constituencies. No party could, however, obtain more mandates on the second count than it had already obtained on the first.[2]

The principle of proportional representation was, however, by no means restricted in its application to the apportionment of mandates and elections to the National Council. A modified system of proportional representation was, for instance, laid down for elections to the Federal Council.[3] And by Article 55 it was decreed that elections to the Chief Committee, the most important organ of the National Council, were to be on a proportional representation basis. Article 95 decreed that members of the Provincial Councils should be elected on a proportional representation basis. Article 119, (2), decreed that proportional representation should be used for elections to municipal councils. Article 119, (4), went so far as to arrange

[1] St. G. Bl. Nr. 115, Article 33. But Kelsen points out that 'Diese Einrichtung hatte schon bei der Beratung der Wahlordnung zur konstituierenden Nationalversammlung viele entschiedene Gegner gefunden u. haben nunmehr alle grossen Parteien dagegen Stellung genommen'. (Kelsen, op. cit, vol. iv, p. 134.)

[2] This restriction was largely abrogated by the Electoral Law of 11 July 1923, in which it was laid down that a party might obtain any number of seats on the second count provided that it had obtained at least one on the first. This Law, however, established four big constituencies for the second count—another instance of the tendency of Austrian constitutionalists to give with one hand while taking away with the other.

That the objections raised to the 1920 arrangement were not merely theoretical is shown by the election results of 1923 and 1930. On both these occasions the German Nationalists gained more seats by the second count than they had already obtained on the first. In 1923 they gained three by the first and seven by the second; in 1930 two by the first and five by the second. (Zurcher, A. J., *The Experiment with Democracy in Central Europe*, Oxford University Press, 1933, p. 82. He quotes figures taken from the *Statistisches Handbuch für die Republik Österreich*, 1923 and 1930.)

[3] The modifications introduced by Article 34, (3), and Article 35, (1), were occasioned in the one case in deference to Christian Socialist federalist views, and in the other by the fear of the Social Democrats that they would remained unrepresented in the more predominantly conservative of the Provinces. Cf. with Weimar Constitution, Article 61.

that if municipal councils chose to elect special administrative committees, such committees must be elected on a proportional representation basis.[1]

Direct government by the people was provided for in the Austrian constitution.[2] It was not, however, intended that frequent use should be made of these provisions. Article 24, for instance, enumerating the various legislative organs of the State, makes no mention of direct legislation by the Initiative and the Referendum. Article 41, (2), provides that every proposal signed by two hundred thousand qualified voters, or by half of the qualified voters in each of three Provinces, must be submitted by the Federal Government to the National Council. It may be observed, however, that the quorum of petitioners is, relatively speaking, a very high one.[3] And it was unlikely that the second of the two conditions would ever be fulfilled, in view of the fact that co-operation between the various Provinces was, as in pre-war days, discouraged.[4]

The Referendum could only be set in motion by the National Council itself.[5]

Only in the case foreseen in Article 44, (2) (a complete revision of the constitution), was a Referendum compulsory; and even in this case the effect of the article seems problematical, since no definition of "complete revision" is provided.

Of the Provinces, only Salzburg, Tyrol, and Vorarlberg included provisions for direct democracy in their constitutions.

[1] Verdier, op. cit., p. 189. It may be noted also that when, in accordance with the Geneva Protocol of 4 October 1922, it became necessary to set up a Council of State endowed with special powers, the third protocol, dealing with this, set up a body composed of the Government and twenty-six councillors who were to be elected on a proportional representation basis.

[1] The provisions were, however, somewhat half-hearted. Most of the Social Democrats did not approve of proportional representation, fearing that it might undermine the supremacy of Parliament. The Christian Socialists, who had at first supported it warmly because of their control over the Provinces, became doubtful in proportion as the question of the proposed administrative reform, which they felt would weaken their hold on the Provinces, became actual.

[3] In Switzerland, for instance, only thirty thousand votes are needed. Swiss Constitution, Article 89.

[4] Cf. Law of 1860 with Article 107, 1920. [5] Article 43.

(ii) *The Federal Principle*

The same criticism may be applied to Article 2 ("Austria is a Federal State") as was applied to Article 1—namely, that it is a judgement rather than a law. Whether or not Austria was a federal State necessarily depended upon subsequent provisions in the constitution. Moreover, as Adamovich points out, the term 'federal State' is susceptible of a variety of interpretations. Kelsen, however, considered that the constitution of October 1920 could be accepted as a *bona fide* federal constitution since it provided for an organ whereby the Provinces could take part in the legislative and administrative work of the State. It differed, he thought, in this respect, from prewar constitutions, although these had contained, in many cases, provisions of a federal nature.

But it is clear that Austria was not a federal State in the sense that there was any question of sovereignty being divided between the State and the Provinces. It was not laid down in so many words that State law takes precedence over provincial law. But the absence of this statement—probably out of deference to the prevalent federalist views—did not mean so much an accretion of strength to the Provinces as an accumulation of work for the Constitutional Court.

In considering how far the federal principle was incorporated in the 1920 constitution it may be convenient to deal first with the extent to which the Provinces participated in federal legislation, since this participation constitutes, as Kelsen points out, the essence of a federal system.

By the 1920 constitution a federal organ, the Federal Council, was set up. The Federal Council was composed of members elected by the Provincial Councils.[1] The Provincial Councils did not, however, return an equal number of members.[2] Again, the provision that the representatives

[1] Article 35.

[2] Article 34. In this respect a compromise was reached between the more extreme of the Christian Socialists who considered that the Provinces, which varied greatly in size, should none the less, as equal sovereign bodies, return an equal number of representatives, and the Social Democrats who wished representation to be on a basis strictly proportional to the population.

elected need not be members of the Provincial Councils, although they should be eligible for such membership, suggests that it was not intended that the Federal Council members should be directly representative of the Provincial Councils.[1] Further, proportional representation was introduced in order to secure representation for the largest of the minority parties in all the Provinces.[2]

The Provinces could not therefore be represented in the Federal Council, as they were in the American Upper House, by corporate bodies of voters. Indeed, the provisions of Article 56, by which it was decreed that members should not be bound by instructions from any outside body, were expressly made to apply also to members of the Federal Council.[3] And these Articles, apart from the fact that they made impossible a strict representation of provincial interests, also constituted a very considerable interference by the State on what might well have been regarded as purely provincial matters.

The influence of the Federal Council on federal legislation was a limited one. It could submit bills to the National Council through the Federal Government,[4] and with certain important exceptions, as, for instance, measures dealing with financial matters, it had a right of suspensive veto. Bills thus vetoed could, however, be repassed by the National Council by a special majority.

It may be said, therefore, that the Federal Council was not organized on a strictly federal basis, and that its powers, as compared with those of the National Council, were extremely limited.

Those legislative powers not specifically enumerated as belonging to the State, were left to the Provinces.[5] Actually,

[1] Article 35, (2).

[2] Article 35, (1), inserted at the instigation of the Social Democrats.

[3] Kelsen comments on this: 'Dass die Mitglieder des Bundesrates nicht an die Aufträge des Landtags gebunden sind, der sie entsendet, ist jedoch darum besonders bemerkenswert, weil es sich beim Bundesrat doch offenbar um eine Vertretung der Länderinteressen handelt. . . . Die Mitglieder des Bundesrates sind daher ebensowenig Vertreter des Landtages oder eines Landes, wie die Mitglieder des Nationalrates Vertreter des Bundesvolkes oder einzelner Wählergruppen sind.' (Op. cit., vol. v, p. 145.)

[4] Article 41, (1).

[5] Article 15, (1).

however, the enumeration of powers belonging to the State covered a very wide range of subjects.

By Article 12 the Provinces had the right to provide supplementary legislation to general laws laid down by the State. If, however, the Provinces did not enact the necessary supplementary legislation within a given period of time, the State could pass the necessary legislation itself.[1] All provincial legislation required the sanction of the Government. Sanction could be refused on the grounds that the law in question endangered federal interests, and the provincial law could only be re-enacted with a special majority.[2] Even then, the case could be brought before the Constitutional Court by the Federal Government, on the grounds that the law in question was unconstitutional.[3] The consent of the State was necessary for any legislation requiring its co-operation.[4]

The legislative rights of the Provinces were therefore not extensive.

They were, however, far more richly endowed with administrative rights.[5] These were of two kinds: (*a*) direct administrative rights—i.e. in connection with administration dealing with exclusively provincial matters; (*b*) indirect administrative

[1] Article 15, (2). [2] Article 98, (2).

[3] But the Provinces could also challenge State laws on the ground of their unconstitutionality. Article 140, (1).

[4] Article 97, (2).

[5] The fourth section of the constitution, Articles 95–120, dealing with legislative and executive administration in the Provinces, required, however, to be implemented by three more laws before it could come into effect. The first of these, governing the financial relationship between the State and the Provinces, was passed on 3 March 1922 (B. G. Bl. Nr. 124). The second and third, dealing with administrative reform in the Provinces and with education, were never passed. Administrative power was divided between the State and the Provinces on the lines laid down by the Law of February 1861; legislative power was divided in accordance with the Law of 1867 (Articles 11 and 12); and educational facilities were provided in accordance with the Law of 1868. This delay was unfortunate in that it served to increase the already existing friction between the State and the Provinces by perpetuating uncertainty in their relationships; and legislation passed in the eighteen-sixties, the heyday of *laissez-faire* liberalism, could not meet adequately the needs of the new Austria. For instance, section 11 of the Law of 1867, enumerating matters to be dealt with by the State legislation, omits all reference to economic and social matters. Moreover, inadequate legislation could not, as it had been in the pre-war period, be implemented by Imperial ordinances.

rights, i.e. administration in connection with federal legislation. It may be noted, however, that, even in connection with direct administrative rights, the State had a certain right to intervene. A Federal Minister could, for instance, challenge a provincial administrative act before the Administrative Court, on the grounds that the interests of the State had been injured thereby.[1] And any person could challenge any administrative act by bringing it before the Administrative Court, on the ground that it was *ultra vires*.

As regards provincial administration which supplemented federal legislation, the control of the State was considerable. And although it was intended to abolish as far as possible the old system of dual administration in the Provinces by using provincial officials for federal administration, it was expressly provided that, if the Provinces failed to implement federal legislation within a given length of time, the State might delegate the necessary administrative powers to its own officials. If supplementary administrative regulations were necessary in more than one Province, and the Provinces concerned could not reach an agreement, federal officials could be put in. Moreover, the Governor, the chief administrative official in the Provinces, although elected by the various Provincial Councils, was sworn in by the President.[2] And when local officials acted for the Federal Government they became, *ipso facto*, federal officials. Thus, the right of appeal against

[1] This was a new provision. In the old Austrian constitution only private persons could appeal against a decision before the Administrative Court. And this provision was the more important in view of the wide powers with which the Administrative Court was endowed. By Article 133, (3), for instance, it was empowered to decide cases on their merits, apart from legal considerations. This was a new departure, although Article 133, (1) and (2), had been taken over from the Laws of 1875. Kelsen comments as follows upon this Article: 'Die Möglichkeit einer Reformation von Verwaltungsakten durch den zentralen Verwaltungsgerichtshof ist um so bedeutungsvoller, wenn man berücksichtigt, dass es sich dabei auch um Verwaltungsakte handelt, die im selbständigen Wirkungsbereich des Landes gesetzt werden, u. dass deren Reformation durch ein Bundesgericht erfolgt.' (Kelsen, *Jahrbuch des öffentlichen Rechts*, vol. xi, p. 263.) On the other hand, the Provinces had indirect control over the appointment of half the members of the Administrative Court (Article 135).

[2] Article 101, (4).

their actions lay through the central authorities and not through the Provincial Assemblies.

It may, therefore, be said that, although the Provinces were endowed with comparatively far-reaching administrative rights and duties, the State had extensive supervisory rights.

As regards judicial rights, Article 82 enunciates the principle that "The whole judicial system lies within the competence of the State".[1] It may, however, be noted that, although the Provinces had no influence over the election of the judges of the ordinary Courts, who were appointed on the advice of the Senates by the Federal Ministry and the President,[2] they had some control over appointments to the Administrative and Constitutional Courts. For instance, by Article 135, the nominations of the Federal Government for the posts of Vice-president, and half the members of the Administrative Court, required the assent of the Federal Council. Article 147 laid down somewhat similar provisions for appointments to the Constitutional Court.[3] But this case differed from the former in that the Federal Council had no influence over the appointment of the Vice-president.

It is clear, however, that the share of the Provinces in the working of the judiciary was even smaller than their share in legislation and administration.

But, while there can be no doubt that the substance of power lay with the State, lip-service was certainly freely paid to the federal idea. The outstanding example of this is Article 2, (1),[4] to which reference has already been made. Another example may be taken from Article 2, (2), where reference is made to the 'independence' of the Provinces. But, as Kelsen points out, this word has no exact legal meaning.[5] Article 15, (1), refers to cases not expressly made over to the State, as remaining within

[1] Kelsen comments on this: 'Dass die gesamte Gerichtsbarkeit dem Bund vorbehalten ist, bedeutet einen, für einen Bundesstaat ungewöhnlichen Grad von Zentralisation.' (Op. cit., vol. v, p. 176.)

[2] Article 86, (1).

[3] In this case, however, the Federal Council was responsible for the actual appointments. It did not merely give its assent to proposals of the Government.

[4] 'Österreich ist ein Bundesstaat.'

[5] Op. cit., vol. v, pp. 66–7.

the sphere of provincial autonomy.[1] But, as the Federal State had in fact evolved from a unitary State, the word 'remain' is meaningless.

By Article 26, (2), it was laid down that the country should be divided up into constituencies within the various Provinces. Apart, however, from the fact that this constituted a recognition of the federal ideal, it is difficult to see that the Provinces derived any particular benefit from this arrangement. Article 36, providing for strict rotation among the Provinces in the office of President of the Federal Council, is of a similar character.

Article 24 announces that legislation shall be by the National Council, together with the Federal Council elected by the Provincial Councils. But in fact, as has been pointed out, the legislative power of the Federal Council was very slight indeed. The Federal Council had, for instance, no share in the appointing of the Government;[2] and it could not even set up special committees of investigation.[3]

Again, by the terms of Article 52, the Federal Council could, as the National Council, inquire into the conduct of the Government. It might be supposed that the corollary of this Article would be that, if the conduct of the Government was found to be unsatisfactory, the Federal Council could take some steps towards its removal. This, however, was not the case.[4]

There were, it is true, certain things which could not be done without the consent of the Federal Council. By Article 3, (2), for instance, it was decreed that no alterations could be made in the boundaries of the Provinces (except as provided by the Peace Treaties), except by agreement of all the Provinces concerned.[5] By Article 35, (4), it was decreed that no alteration

[1] 'Verbleibt sie im selbständigen Wirkungsbereich der Länder.' This terminology may be compared with that of the previous draft of this article, 'Die Länder . . . übertragen dem Bund', etc. The implication of these phrases is that the Provinces were originally sovereign bodies. This was certainly not the case. (Kelsen, op. cit., vol. v, p. 80.)

[2] Article 70. [3] Article 53, (1). [4] Article 74, (1).

[5] Cf. Weimar Constitution, Article 18, which empowers the State, in certain circumstances, to alter boundaries without the consent of the Provinces concerned.

should be made in the constitution of the Federal Council without its assent. And assent required a majority vote in favour from the representatives of at least four Provinces. A minority of the Provinces could thus prevent an amendment.[1]

Finally, by Article 132, if a Province were involved in a dispute before the Administrative Court, the case had, as a rule, to be tried by a Senate having among its members a judge who formerly belonged to the judicial or administrative service of that Province.[2]

But although certain actions could not be carried through without the consent of the Provinces, effective precautions were taken to ensure that the Provinces should never become overpowerful.

Articles 95–120, for instance, gave the State control over the political and social structure of the Provinces. The provisions ensuring democratic government, safeguarding minority rights, and guaranteeing to the State extensive supervisory rights, guarded against the possibility of the growth of a strong, united opposition to the central Government from reactionary parties in the Provinces. The extent to which State control over the Provinces went may be seen by Article 100, which provided that a Provincial Council could be dissolved by the Government, if the consent of the Federal Council was obtained.[3] The Article provides an example of the spirit of compromise which pervades the Austrian constitution, for, while the federal principle is undermined by the provision that a Provincial Assembly can be dissolved by a State organ, it is safeguarded by the provision that the assent of the highest federal organ shall be necessary for such a dissolution.

The Administrative and the Constitutional Courts were clearly intended as State organs (although, as has been pointed

[1] The provisions of this article should have been applied also to Article 34 (dealing with representation of the Provinces in the *Bundresat*). Originally Articles 34 and 35 were one. When they were separated the constitutional committee omitted to make Article 35, (4), apply to both of them, though it was clearly far more important that it should apply to Article 34.

[2] Cf. with provisions for trying cases before the Permanent Court of International Justice (Statute of the Court, Article 31).

[3] The consenting vote, however, required a quorum of one-half of the members, and a two-thirds majority.

out, the Provinces exercised a certain indirect control over the appointment of their personnel). For instance, if a federal minister considered that the interests of the State had been injured by an erroneous decree of a provincial authority, he could bring the matter before the Administrative Court. No such provision, however, was made for appeals by provincial ministers against State decrees.[1]

Finally, the following provisions may be noted, which though not themselves of great importance, none the less indicate the general tendency to ignore the federal principle. By Article 41, (2), for instance, voters in three different Provinces could join in submitting an Initiative, provided that in each Province half of the qualified voters agreed to it. This was to be an alternative to an Initiative signed by two hundred thousand of the qualified voters in one Province, and was intended to safeguard the rights of minorities in the smaller Provinces. It was clearly, however, an infringement of the federal principle.[2]

Finally, the formula used in the publication of laws is "The National Council has decided . . .", etc. (If the law is passed

[1] Article 129, (2). This may be compared with Article 140, (1), regulating appeals to the Constitutional Court. In this case the right of appeal is guaranteed both to the State and to the Provinces.

It may be noted that in the important sphere of finance, the control of the State was to be even further extended, by the Finance Constitutional Law of 3 March 1922 (B. G. Bl. Nr. 124). If a proposed provincial law dealing with financial matters was vetoed by the Federal Government, its re-passage by the Province concerned, with a special majority, did not settle the matter. 'In diesem Falle kann nämlich die Bundesregierung den Einspruch trotz des Wiederholungsbeschlusses aufrechterhalten. Der dadurch entstandene Konflikt zwischen Bundesregierung u. Landesgesetzgebung wird durch einen ständigen gemeinsamen Ausschuss des Nationalrates u. des Bundesrates entschieden. Dieser hat nämlich zu beschliessen, ob der Einspruch aufrecht zu bleiben hat, oder nicht. Entscheidet sich der Ausschuss für den Einspruch der Bundesregierung, erhält deren Veto einen absoluten Charakter.' (Kelsen, *Jahrbuch des öffentlichen Rechts*, vol. xi, p. 258.)

[2] This article may be compared with Article 15, (3). In this case, the Provinces must co-operate in the passage of supplementary legislation under Articles 11 and 12. If they fail to do so, the right to pass such legislation is transferred to the federal minister. These two articles might seem to conflict with Article 107. But Article 107 is probably intended to prevent a combination of Provinces hostile to the central Government (cf. with Imperial Decree of 1860). Co-operation between the Provinces was not, on the whole, encouraged. By Article 107, for instance, Provincial Councils were forbidden to communicate with one another, except in matters falling within their autonomous sphere of action.

as the result of a Referendum this is noted.) No mention is made of the co-operation of the Federal Council. Laws are dated in the Federal Law Book from the day of their third reading by the National Council.

(iii) *The National Council*

The Austrian State was reorganized by the constitution of 1920 as a democratic, federal, and parliamentary republic. The pivot of the whole political structure was the National Council.

The sovereignty of the National Council was ensured by the almost complete absence of provisions for its control either by the people who elected it, the Federal Council, the Government, or the President.

From the first of these possible controlling bodies the National Council was virtually divorced after it had been elected. It was specifically laid down in Article 56 that members should not be bound by instructions. The people could, it is true, introduce legislation directly, by the device of the Initiative. They were not, however, encouraged to do so; the numbers of supporters required for an Initiative motion was, as has been pointed out, comparatively high; nor was the National Council bound to pass such bills. Similarly, proposals involving a complete revision of the federal constitution had to be submitted to a Referendum. But no attempt was made to define what was meant by a 'complete revision'; and again, it was not stated that the National Council was bound by the result of such a Referendum. Other measures only had to be submitted to a Referendum if the National Council so decided.[1] The National Council could only be dissolved before the end of its four-year term of office by its own decree. If it was so dissolved, it had to be reassembled by its President, if a quarter of its members so requested.[2]

But, if the National Council was not controlled by its electors, still less was it controlled by the Federal Council. The Federal Council had, as has been pointed out, in a few

[1] Article 43. [2] Article 28.

isolated and comparatively unimportant instances an absolute veto; in the majority of cases it had a suspensive veto,[1] and in a small number of extremely important cases, concerned with financial matters, it had no veto at all.[2] It had little control over the Government. It could, as the National Council, inquire into the Government's conduct of business.[3] But it could not, by a withdrawal of confidence, cause the dismissal of the Government.[4] In any case, it was possible for the National Council to exercise an indirect control over its composition, because, owing to a mistake in drafting, the Federal Council did not possess an absolute veto right in regard to alterations to Article 34, dealing with representation of the Provinces in the Federal Council. Provided that the requisite majority could be obtained in the Federal Council, the Government, which was the tool of the National Council, could dissolve a Provincial Council and thereby remove its representatives from the Upper House.

The President, whose functions were not intended to be other than decorative, was elected by the Federal Assembly;[5] the National Council could take the initiative in calling the Federal Assembly together to impeach him.[6] He was the servant of the National Council, not its master.

But the sovereignty of the National Council comes to the fore most clearly in the provisions made to ensure its control over the Government. Article 70, (1), decrees that the Government shall be chosen by the National Council, voting upon the proposal laid before it by the Chief Committee.[7]

[1] Article 42, (4). [2] Article 42, (5). [3] Article 52
[4] Article 74, (1). [5] Article 60. [6] Article 63, (2).
[7] 'Die Bundesregierung wird vom Nationalrat in namentlicher Abstimmung auf einen vom Hauptausschuss zu erstattenden Gesamtvorschlag gewählt.' This article might, however, suggest that the National Council had a more absolute control over the personnel of the Government than was actually the case. By Article 72, (2), for instance, it was stipulated that the list of ministers should be countersigned by the new Chancellor. Therefore, in fact, this meant that the Chancellor chose his own colleagues although his choice was subject to the approval of the National Council. Kelsen remarks: 'Die . . . Bestimmung, dass der neugewählte Bundeskanzler die Bestellungsurkunden aller Mitglieder der Regierung gegenzuzeichnen hat, hat praktisch die grosse Bedeutung, dass kein Mitglied des neuen Kabinettes gegen oder ohne den Willen des präsumtiven Bundeskanzlers berufen werden kann.' (*Die Verfassungsgesetze der Republik Österreich*, vol. v, p. 168.)

Article 70, (3), provided for the eventuality of a Governmen resigning while the National Council was not in session. I this case, a new Government had to be chosen provisionally b the Chief Committee. As soon as the National Council re assembled, the election of the Government had to take plac as usual.[1]

Members of the Federal Government were responsible to th National Council while in office,[2] and impeachment proceed ings could be brought against them.[3] The Government coul be questioned on all matters relating to the execution of th laws by members of both Houses. Both Houses could expres their wishes in regard to the exercise of the executive power by resolution.[4] And it was even laid down by Article 55 tha in addition laws could be introduced providing that particula ordinances of the Government should require the assent of th Chief Committee. The presence of the Government could b demanded by either House, and by the committees.[5]

Another means of control by the National Council over th Government was the Independent Court of Audit. This cour was responsible for drafting the balance-sheet of the Budge and presenting it to the National Council. It could examin the expenditure of every agency of the Federal State. It coul be entrusted with the right to examine the expenditure of an enterprise in which the Federal State was financially interested.[6] And by Article 122, (1), it was expressly laid down that th Independent Court of Audit was directly responsible to th National Council.[7]

Finally, by Article 74, (1), it was decreed that if the Nationa Council, by express resolution, withdrew its confidence from

[1] This provision, safeguarding the power of the National Council, had no been included in the constitution of 14 March 1919.

[2] Article 76. [3] Article 142, (2), b. [4] Article 52.

[5] Article 75. On the other hand, members of the Government could tak part in debates in the National Council, the Federal Council, and the com mittees (except debates in the Chief Committee, to which they had to b specially invited). They had always to be heard if they wished to speak.

[6] Article 121.

[7] The president of this court was elected by the National Council o proposal of the Chief Committee, Article 122, (3). He could be dismissed b resolution of the National Council, Article 123, (2).

he Federal Government, or from individual members of the Government, they would be thereby removed from office.[1] It vas not, however, intended that this weapon should be lightly mployed against a Government, for it was stipulated that uch a resolution would require a quorum of half the members of the National Council. And, if one-fifth of the members so lemanded, the vote could be postponed for two days.[2] The Government, apart from this somewhat meagre stipulation, ad no means of protecting itself against an adverse vote by a hance coalition in the National Council, since it could not confront the National Council with the choice between continued support and a dissolution.

As has been pointed out, the National Council had practically complete control over all legislation. It had also considerable executive functions. By Article 50, political and certain other treaties required for their validity the consent of he National Council. By Article 53, it was empowered to set up by resolution Committees of Inquiry,[3] before which all public authorities were obliged to give evidence if required. By Article 54 certain executive duties were specifically made over to the National Council, such as the fixing of the prices of uch federal services as railways; the fixing of the prices of monopoly goods; and the fixing of the salaries of persons employed by the State. Apart from these specified cases, it was laid down in Article 55 that the National Council should share n the executive power of the State through its Chief Committee, to which reference has already been made. Kelsen has lescribed this body as the most important political organ of the National Council.[4] Provision had been made for its election n the constitution of 14 March 1919. Its membership had hen been fixed at eleven, whereas by the constitution of 1920

[1] It may be noted that, since it was anticipated that the dismissal of an ndividual minister by a vote of no confidence should not necessarily involve he resignation of the whole ministry, the cabinet system was not adopted.

[2] Kelsen comments on this: 'Dass die Wirkung des Misstrauensvotums erfassungsgesetzlich ausdrücklich normiert wird, ist eine Besonderheit nserer Verfassung' (op. cit., vol. v, p. 169).

[3] Cf. with Article 34 of the German Constitution, according to which such committee had to be set up if one-fifth of members so demanded.

[4] *Jahrbuch des öffentlichen Rechts*, vol. xi, p. 246.

the number of members was not specified. And the Presiden of the National Council was no longer *ex officio* a member anc Chairman of the Committee. The Chairman was now electec by the Committee itself. The Chief Committee was elected by the National Council from among its own members, on a basi of proportional representation of all parties.[1]

Finally, the control exercised by the National Council ove the judiciary was considerable. By Article 86, (1), it was decreec that the judges should be appointed upon nomination by the Federal Government.[2] The control exercised by the Nationa Council over the Federal Government has just been pointec out. That exercised by it over the Independent Court of Audi has also been referred to. The President and half the member of the Administrative Court were appointed by the Federa Government upon nomination by the Chief Committee.[3] The President, Vice-president, and half of the members and deputy members of the Constitutional Court were elected by the National Council.[4]

It may be said, therefore, that by the constitution of Octobe 1920, Austria was reconstructed as a democratic, federal, anc parliamentary State, the pivot of which was intended to be the National Council.

(iv) *Conclusions*

The chief criticism that can be levelled at the 1920 constitu- tion is the weak position in which its provisions placed the Government, the proper authority of which was deliberately undermined, mainly because of the fear of a return to the old too powerful rule of the executive. The fact that the right to demand a dissolution was withheld from the Government together with the fact that, owing to the introduction of pro-

[1] It may be noted that, although the National Council exercised no direc control over the Provinces, it did exercise very considerable indirect control through its control of the Government.

[2] With regard to this article, it may be noted that although the senate were required to produce proposals for such appointments, these proposal were not, as they were in the project of 22 November 1918, made binding on the Government.

[3] Article 135. [4] Article 147, (2).

portional representation, it would probably not often be possible for a Government to rely upon a safe majority, meant that its position was unlikely to be a strong one. And it was clearly improbable that such a Government would be in a position to pursue a coherent policy. It would be bound to consider the probable reaction of each part of its programme upon the various parties on whose support it was dependent, and even if it had not made definite promises to exclude certain policies and include others, such considerations would probably necessitate the pursuit of largely negative and often inconsistent policies.

The evils which ensued could have been foreseen, for it was clear from the beginning that the future well-being of Austria would depend upon the capacity of her rulers to pursue a firm policy of reconstruction over a period of years, unhampered by the exigencies of party politics. Moreover, the danger to be feared from an unduly powerful Government could have been obviated had it been made clear that, as in England, the Government was simply the executive committee of the Lower House. But the Austrian constitution provided that although members of the Government must be eligible for election to the Lower House, they need not actually be members of it.[1] The evils which inevitably ensued from this deliberately manufactured weakness of the executive gradually operated to bring the whole theory of democratic government into disrepute in Austria.

The second criticism which may be levelled at the 1920 constitution was the ill-advised introduction of proportional representation. Although, as has been pointed out, one consequence of this was certainly to make possible a tighter control by the National Council over the Government than had been intended, it had also the effect of weakening the National Council itself, for this became as a house divided against itself, a battleground for rival groups. And the battle was not only fierce, but also futile, for the closed list system,

[1] Article 70, (2). Having separated the two bodies, a characteristic attempt was made to link them up again, through the Chief Committee of the Lower House.

which had been introduced as the concomitant of proportional representation, meant that members to a large extent ceased to be free agents, and tended to act under the dictates of their respective party caucuses. The activity of the National Council was the more arid in that there was no possibility of its being either suspended or dissolved before the expiration of its term of office, except by its own volition. Thus in fact sovereignty lay not in the Lower House, but in an indeterminate body of persons, frequently unknown to and certainly not elected by the people, in whose hands lay the control of the party machinery.

As far as central Government went, Austria was thus provided by the 1920 constitution with a weak Government, an irresponsible Lower House, and a powerless electorate. This weakness at the centre naturally made itself felt throughout the whole organization of the State. A central authority so constituted could not have hoped to exert control over the dissatisfied and recalcitrant Provinces—nor could it ever have given the country as a whole the lead that was so urgently needed.

A third defect in the 1920 constitution, the removal of which might have obviated to some extent the first two, lay in the lack of power accorded to the Upper House. This omission was the more unnecessary in that the constitution laid down carefully the conditions regulating election to the Upper House; and they were such that there would have been little danger that the Upper House would have constituted a stronghold of particularist tendencies, in permanent opposition to the central Government. In fact, it appeared likely that the Upper House would, on the whole, share the political views of the Lower House. Had it been made permissible for the Upper House in certain circumstances to force a dissolution, as was the case in England before the passage of the Parliament Act, some safeguard would have existed against the danger of a Lower House continuing in office, and exerting its sway over Governments who were its puppets, after it had lost the confidence of the electorate.

The implication of certain articles is not clear. Article 9, for instance, enunciates the principle that 'the generally recognized rules of International Law form part of the law of the State'. This may mean, as Kelsen points out,[1] rules which are everywhere accepted—in which case the provision seems superfluous—or it may mean rules recognized by the majority of nations.[2] The meaning of Article 83, (3), also appears to be uncertain. Kelsen suggests that it may mean that extraordinary courts may not be set up to deal with individual cases, but only with classes of cases.

There are many cases of inaccuracy in drafting. Thus, for instance, Article 19, (1), mentions the President, the ministers, and the members of the provincial Governments as being elected commissioners of the people, who may be held responsible before the Constitutional Court. But the list of officials mentioned is not exhaustive;[3] and the Secretaries of State who are included in it could not in fact be held responsible, for they were answerable solely to their individual ministers.

The enumeration in Article 38 of the functions of the Federal Assembly was incomplete.[4] But Kelsen suggests that the omission is explained by the fact that it was not thought desirable to lay too much stress on its right to inquire into the work of, and, if necessary, prosecute, the President, and that the enumeration of this function was therefore deliberately omitted.[5]

In conclusion, it may be said that the failure of parliamentary democracy in Austria was implicit in the constitution of 1920, for this embodied devices such as proportional representation and the closed list, which almost always militate against the successful working of a democratic constitution, especially in politically backward states. And, apart from this, the constitution was probably too elaborate to be worked satisfactorily by a people inexperienced in self-government. It was also extremely expensive, in the number of officials required to work it, for so small a state as Austria.

[1] Op. cit., vol. v, p. 76.

[2] Cf. Article 4 of German Constitution. In the case of Austria it may be observed that whereas by a generally accepted rule of International Law, treaties are valid if they are ratified by the head of a State, according to Article 50, such treaties require the consent of the National Council.

[3] See Article 142, (2), c and d.

[4] Cf. Articles 63, (1), and 68.

[5] *Die Verfassungsgesetze der Republik Österreich*, vol. v, p. 108.

IV

THE REFORM OF THE CONSTITUTION

(i) *The* 1925 *Reforms*

BY 1925, when it was found necessary to introduce various alterations into the constitution of 1920, most of the defects to which attention has been drawn had become apparent. But the reforms of 1925 were, generally speaking, occasioned by administrative exigencies. No radical changes were introduced.

The division of legislative and administrative functions between the State and the Provinces as envisaged by Articles 10–15 of the 1920 constitution had not been at once effected, as it was felt that it would be more satisfactory to wait until three further measures had been passed, dealing respectively with the financial relationship between the State and the Provinces;[1] their respective functions regarding education, and a measure introducing a general reform of provincial administration.

The existing framework of local government was not well adapted to bear the strain of the 1920 constitution for, whereas in the pre-war period the greater part of provincial administration had been within the sphere of the State officials, while the provincial officials had been mainly concerned with legislative matters, this position was reversed by the Articles 10–15 of the 1920 constitution. The smaller and less well-organized group of provincial officials would thus have had to bear the strain of enormously increased duties, while the work of the Governor and the State officials would have been considerably curtailed. It was also hoped that the costly dual administrative system could be abolished before the new arrangements set out in Articles 10–15 came into force.

It was anticipated that these three measures would be passed within a few months. But although a bill regulating the

[1] This measure was passed on 3 March 1922. B. G. Bl. Nr. 124.

financial relationship of the State and the Provinces was passed on 3 March 1922,[1] it was found to be impossible to reach agreement on the other two proposed measures. The effects of the delay became increasingly serious, for the law of 1867, which was still in force as a temporary measure, restricted the legislative activity of the State to a minimum. This measure had been introduced in an era of economic liberalism, and it had already, by the end of the nineteenth century, been found necessary to disregard the limits set by it to State activity. Had these limits been rigidly adhered to, it would have been impossible, for instance, for the State to introduce any social legislation at all. But whereas before the war it had been possible to disregard the 1867 measure with comparative impunity, this was no longer the case in the post-war period, for, with the additional power given by the 1920 constitution to the Constitutional Court, it was always possible that one of the Provincial Governments would challenge even existing legislation as unconstitutional. And the overriding authority of the Emperor was no longer available for forcing through necessary measures. It was therefore considered advisable in 1925 to introduce the new provisions contained in Articles 10–15 of the 1920 constitution without further delay.[2]

Certain reforms were made in the existing system of provincial administration, which were intended to facilitate the working of the new administrative provisions and to prepare the way for a more comprehensive reform in the future. For instance, an attempt was made to end the dual administrative system. Since the war, both the provincial and the state officials (*Bezirkshauptmannschaften*) were indirectly under the control of the Provincial Governments,[3] the only difference being that in the latter case there existed a right of appeal to the Federal Government. Some doubt had, however, existed

[1] B. G. Bl. Nr. 124

[2] Certain minor changes of a centralist character were introduced at the same time, e.g. more control was accorded to the State in matters regarding water and electricity (B. G. Bl. 268, Article 10, x).

[3] For the Provincial Governments assumed, since the war, responsibility for the appointment of the Provincial Governors to whom the State officials were responsible.

regarding the status of those officials whose work was concerned with both indirect and State administration, and with provincial administration. Now they were all declared provincial officials, and a new official, the *Landesamtsdirektor*, appointed by the Provincial Government, with the approval of the Federal Government, was placed at the head of all the officials in each Province.[1] Traces of the old dual system remained, however, for the erstwhile State officials, although now responsible solely to provincial authorities, continued to enjoy their old status as State officials, and attempts to alter this somewhat anomalous state of affairs came to nothing, owing to opposition from two of the three parties of the Government coalition.

Certain minor reforms were introduced at the same time which were designed to strengthen the three control organs of the constitution.

The most important of these reforms was that by which some control over provincial finances was accorded to the Court of Audit.[2] The measure was disapproved of by the federalists, and was only passed under pressure from the League Commissioner. At the same time, the previous position, by which the Court of Audit had acted as a control on the Government, was in some measure reversed. This was also a result of pressure from the League Commissioner, who was anxious both to strengthen the position of the Government, since this body was as a rule ready to co-operate with him, and to induce the Court of Audit to co-operate in carrying through League reforms.

Another important provision passed at that time was that by which the State was accorded the right of absolute veto on provincial taxation for the period from 13 August 1925 to 31 December 1930. Again, the influence of the League Commissioner is clearly perceptible.

[1] B. G. Bl. 268, Article 106.

[2] B. G. Bl. 268, Article 127. Such control has been optional according to the terms of the 1920 constitution (Article 127), and only Burgenland had made use of it. The result had been that the Provincial Governments had been able to nullify the economies imposed by the League on the Federal Government. The Provinces were, however, induced to see reason at the *Länderkonferenz* of 1925.

(ii) *The* 1929 *Reforms*

The period between the 1925 reforms and the very much more radical alterations introduced into the constitution in 1929, was characterized by a steady deterioration of the internal political situation.

By 1929 dissatisfaction with the existing régime had reached a climax. It had already been found necessary to introduce six minor reforms,[1] and, as the 1920 constitution was still not working satisfactorily, desire for a more radical change began to be voiced.

The demand was put forward with the greatest insistence by members of the *Heimwehr*, who openly proclaimed their intention to be the supersession of the existing system of parliamentary democracy by a dictatorship on the general lines of the Italian model.[2]

The desire for reform was not, however, confined to members of the *Heimwehr* movement. It was, for instance, energetically sponsored by the *Landbund.*[3] The movement was also warmly supported by the vast majority of the Christian Socialists, although opinion within the party differed considerably as to what precise measures should be taken. Certain sections in the Provinces, for instance, disapproved strongly of the centralist part of Schober's programme.[4] And peasant opinion feared

[1] *Jahrbuch des öffentlichen Rechts*, vol. xviii, 1930, p. 130.

[2] 'Die Heimwehren forderten, u. fordern noch jetzt, der Ersetzung der parlamentarischen Demokratie durch eine berufsständische Organisation in Verbindung mit einer Art Führerdiktatus, ohne jedoch, diese Forderung im einzelnen zu konkretisieren.' (Kelsen, op. cit., vol. xviii, p. 1930.)

[3] The *Landbund*, however, repudiated strenuously the Social Democrats' accusation that it was working for the installation of a fascist régime. See article in the *Landbund* organ, *Die Stunde*, 20 September 1929: 'Er deckt sich in keiner Weise mit jener rein fascistischen Verfassung, die im Schosse der extremen Kreise der Selbstschutzverbände ausgearbeitet wurde, u. die mit einer vollständigen Beseitigung der demokratischen Verfassung der Republik Osterreich gleichbedeutend wäre. Der Landbund will keineswegs eine fascistische Regierungsform in Österreich installieren, er will nur in manchen, freilich sehr wichtigen Punkten, die gegenwärtige österreichische Verfassung im Sinne einer Stärkung der Staatsautorität abändern.' It seems doubtful, however, whether much reliance should be placed on this statement. The policy of the *Landbund* was a somewhat uncertain one. (See *Manchester Guardian*, 15 October 1929.)

[4] *The Times*, 19 October 1930.

that concentration on constitutional reform might deflect attention from the need for energetic economic measures.[1] There was also a sharp division of opinion between the more moderate members of the party, led by Kunschak, who would probably have liked to see a *rapprochemeut* with the Social Democrats and the right-wing leaders led by Seipel.

The German Nationalists had been advocating reform for many years, as they hoped thereby to bring the Austrian constitution more into line with that of the Reich.

Most of the Social Democrats were probably not opposed to a moderate measure of reform,[2] although in their opinion disarmament was a far more pressing need.[3]

The great difficulty was, however, to reconcile the aims of the moderates of both parties with those of the extremists, who wanted rather to destroy than to reform.

There can be little doubt that a great deal of the disorder in the public life of Austria did lie, as Schober and his followers maintained, in the weakness of the executive. This weakness was in part the inevitable result of the particular circumstances in which the country was placed in the post-war years; economic distress, foreign control, party quarrels, certainly played their part. But all these difficulties might have been overcome, or at least would not have been felt so acutely, had it not been for inherent defects in the constitution of October 1920.

The reasons which prompted the Austrians to mistrust the power of the Government at that time have already been discussed. But, just as they did not foresee in 1920 the difficulties in which this arrangement would involve them, so in 1929 they did not fully realize to what ultimate cause those difficul-

[1] *Frankfurter Zeitung*, 14 September 1929. The Lower Austrian *Bauernbund* —one of the strongest groups within the party—was especially insistent upon this danger. The Social Democrats agreed, see *Frankfurter Zeitung*, 23 October 1929, report of a speech of Renner. 'Wir glauben nicht, aber, dass der Wirtschaft am meisten gedient wird, wenn durch einen rechtzeitigen u. raschen reformierischen Umbau unseres Staates u. unseres politischen Lebens der Keim der Unruhe u. der Spannungen entfernt wird.'

[2] *Manchester Guardian*, 9 September 1929.

[3] Renner, speech on first reading of the bill, reported in *Frankfurter Zeitung*, 23 October 1929.

ties were due. The reformers of 1929 mistook effects for causes.

It was, for instance, widely felt that one of the great evils in the post-war Austrian state had been the politicizing of every department of public life.[1] This was certainly true. But it was not realized that the cause of this lay to a great extent in the constitution itself. The Government had been deliberately placed under the control of the National Council; and instead of being regarded as the executive committee of that body, it had come to be considered as a weak, but potentially dangerous, rival, whose powers must be curtailed at all costs.

The National Council possessed all the necessary constitutional means to enforce its authority. But it was itself controlled by the party leaders as, owing to the system of proportional representation and the closed list, these had almost absolute control over its members. Thus the proper organs of control—the electorate, the National Council, and the Government—had been in the hands of an irresponsible group of men, many of whom were possibly not even known to the Austrian public.[2] For twelve years the party system had thus run riot in Austria, and in consequence many people had come to believe that it was a system inherently vicious, and to advocate its supersession, and the substitution of some non-party form of organization in its stead. But in fact, different parties are simply the organized expression of differences of opinion among the electorate, and as such they are a necessary concomitant of any democratic government. Their abolition may temporarily hide such differences, but can hardly eradicate them. And, if differences cannot be voiced constitutionally, they may

[1] 'Tatsächlich ergab sich auf Grund dieser Verfassung im Verlauf der vergangenen zehn Jahre eine Ueberpolitisierung unseres gesamten Lebens, eine Diktatur des Parteiwesens, dessen Einfluss weit über den politischen Bereich hinaus greift u. so ziemlich alle Gebiete des wirtschaftlichen wie des geistigen Lebens erfasst hat. (*Neues Wiener Tageblatt*, 22 September 1929.)

[2] The disadvantages of the closed-list system were, however, beginning to be understood, and the need for a closer connection between electors and elected urged. 'Tatsächlich wurden die Volksvertreter in ihrer Überzahl nichtmehr vom Volke gewählt, sondern von den Parteiführer, den Parteisekretariaten nominiert.' (*Neues Wiener Tageblatt*, 21 September 1929.) For the same reason large electoral districts were now deprecated. In the end, however, the electoral system remained unchanged.

well find a more dangerous outlet. The parties were not the villains of the piece—but the constitution, by which they were accorded a disproportionate amount of power.

Distrust of the National Council was manifested on all sides. The parties of the right hoped to undermine its power by strengthening the office of President; the Social Democrats, by a more frequent use of the Referendum.[1] In fact, it transpired in the course of the 1929 debates on constitutional reform, that the Social Democrats had revised their views on constitutional questions almost as much as their rivals, the Christian Socialists. Renner, for instance, in the debate on the first reading, remarked that the great weakness of the 1920 constitution had been the concentration of power in the Lower House, to the exclusion of all other bodies.[2] For this reason he announced his approval of the proposals made for strengthening the position of the Government and the President.[3] It is true that Renner was very much more conservative in his views than the majority of the Social Democrats. But the party leaders as a whole were well aware that they were on the defensive, and they did not therefore show themselves averse from reasonable compromise.

One result of the over-politicizing of public life, to which attention had frequently been drawn in the past by Dr. Zimmermann, had been a tendency to multiply officials, and thus to increase the cost of government.[4] Attempts to check

[1] Their proposal was that every bill taken up by Parliament should be submitted to a Referendum if one-third of the National Council advised it, or if 300,000 electors demanded it. (See *Pester Lloyd*, 10 October 1930.)

[2] 'Das ist die erste grosse u. tragische Schwäche unserer geltenden Verfassung, dass sie nicht ein Gleichgewicht hergestellt hat unter den mehreren Trägern der staatlichen Autorität, sondern dass sie alles auf eine Karte gesetzt hat, dass sie den Staat u. seine Ordnung, seine Sicherheit u. Freiheit auf die eine Säule des allmächtigen Parlaments aufbauen wollte. . . . Die Verfassungsnovelle ist vor allem charakterisiert durch das Bemühen, das alte demokratische Ideal der Gewalttrennung durchzuführen.' (*Stenographisches Protokoll*, 102 Sitzung, 22 October 1929.)

[3] 'Es soll vor allem die Bundesregierung in ihrer Position gestärkt werden. Das geschieht schon dadurch, dass der Bundespräsident sie ernennt. Der vorliegende Entwurf hält die Mitte zwischen der Präsidenten-Republik u. der Parlamentarischen-Republik; ich glaube eine gesunde u. richtige Mitte' (op. cit.).

[4] *Neues Wiener Abendblatt*, 18 September 1929. Schober pointed out that Austria, a country of seven million persons, had seven hundred members of legislative bodies, (*Reichspost*, 20 October 1929.)

the growth of federalism, and so simplify the structure of government, had actually contributed further to this end.[1] The number of officials was to some extent curtailed by the 1929 reforms. The National Council was reduced from one hundred and sixty-five to one hundred and twenty members,[2] and the Provincial Councils were limited in proportion to the number of citizens in the Province.[3] The cost of administration in general was cut down. But Schober announced after the passage of the Bill that he was still far from satisfied in this respect. The fact that the constitution of 1920 was, in any case, too expensive and too complicated to be worked satisfactorily by a people inexperienced in the art of self-government was not, however, generally grasped,[4] and the constitution emerged after the reforms if anything more complicated than it had been before.

One of the chief aims of the reforms was to strengthen the executive. The power of the President, hitherto little more than a figurehead, was therefore greatly extended, chiefly at the expense of the National Council.[5] Schober made use of the suggestions put forward by the Pan-Germans at Salzburg in 1920, by the Christian Socialists since the beginning of 1928, and by the *Landbund* in a memorandum addressed to Steeruwitz on 31 August 1929.[6] In the main the new proposals followed the German model. The President's term of office was extended from four to six years; and direct election was substituted for indirect. The Christian Socialists maintained firmly that this was the more democratic method.[7] The device

[1] Thirteen different kinds of jurisdiction were now recognized, instead of the four envisaged by the constitution of 1920. Kelsen remarks that 'die Folge davon . . . ist, dass die Verteilung der Kompetenzen zwischen Bund u. Ländern ein überaus kompliziertes Bild der verschiedensten Rechtsfiguren zeigt'. (*Jahrbuch des öffentlichen Rechts*, vol. xviii, pp. 133–4.)

[2] A result of the restriction of the franchise to those over twenty-one years of age.

[3] B. G. Bl. Nr. 393, Article 95, (4).

[4] The Social Democrats, for instance, proposed a wider use of the Referendum, by which every bill should be submitted to the people, if one-third of the National Council so desired, or if 300,000 electors so requested. (*Pester Lloyd*, 10 October 1929.)

[5] Articles 60–7. The idea of a strong government was still suspect.

[6] Malbone W. Graham, 'Constitutional Crisis in Austria', *American Political Science Review*, vol. 24, 1930.

[7] *Reichspost*, 22 October 1929. Seipel, ibid., 19 October 1929.

adopted was, however, not unexceptionable. Election was compulsory and, if no candidate succeeded in gaining an absolute majority in the first count, only the two parties having the largest number of votes in the first count could nominate candidates for the second. Since these could then nominate new candidates there was nothing to prevent parties that had gained a large number of votes, by putting up moderate candidates, from confronting the people with extremists in the second count.[1]

The power of the President over the Government and the National Council was considerable. The President, and not the Chief Committee, now appointed the former, although the confidence of the National Council was still necessary.[2] The President could dissolve the National Council, with the assent of the Government. But he could only do this once for the same reason; and fresh elections had to be held within ninety days.[3] During this period, however, the Government could carry on in virtue of its right to issue ordinances.[4]

In general, the principle of parliamentary rule was much weakened by the fact that it was now assumed that Parliament was not a permanent body. The President had to assemble it in the spring and the autumn. It was laid down that the spring sitting should last for at least two months, but that it could not continue after 15 June. The autumn session had to be for at least four months, but it could not begin until after 15 October.[5] It was envisaged as a possibility, therefore, that the National Council would not be in session for more than six months of the year. Committees could, however, be entrusted with carrying on the work when it was not in session.[6] And it was provided that it should be reassembled should a third of the Upper or Lower House so demand. In this case, it had to be summoned within two weeks for an extraordinary session.[7]

The power of the National Council over the budget also

[1] The original proposal had been that the President should be directly elected, but that the verdict might be revised by the two legislative chambers. (*The Times*, 15 October 1929.)
[2] Articles 70, (2), and 74, (1). [3] Article 29.
[4] Article 18, (3). [5] Article 28, (1). [6] Article 28, (4).
[7] Article 28, (2).

declined. The original proposal had been that, if the budget were not voted at the right time, the provisions of the previous year should hold good. Eventually, however, this period was limited to eight weeks.[1]

The corollary of these limitations placed upon the power of the hitherto omnipotent National Council was the legislative power now entrusted to the President. Kelsen remarks, for instance, on the importance of the new ordinance right.[2] This innovation was regarded with the deepest suspicion by the Social Democrats, who saw in it an attempt to resuscitate the famous Paragraph 14 of Imperial days. Schober, however, solemnly asserted that nothing of this kind was intended. He pointed out that it had been found necessary to entrust the executive with the right to issue ordinances in certain circumstances in most other democratic countries, as France, England, Ireland, Czechoslovakia, etc. The Social Democrats, however, wanted this power to be made over to the Chief Committee and liberal opinion disapproved strongly of the whole arrangement.[3] Eventually, a compromise was reached by which all ordinances issued by the President required the immediate assent of a sub-committee of the Chief Committee, and the assent, within a month, of the National Council, which had to be summoned to consider them within eight days.[4] Ordinances could not change constitutional laws, impose permanent financial burdens, or alienate State property. It was further provided that ordinances should only be issued in

[1] Article 51, (3).

[2] Kelsen, *Jahrbuch des öffentlichen Rechts*, vol. xviii, p. 141: 'Im innigsten Zusammenhang mit der Einschränkung der Parlamentsfunktion steht die sehr einschneidende Reform, die das Verordnungsrecht einführt.'

[3] *Frankfurter Zeitung*, 10 October 1929: 'Die Minorität würde so stets unter Druck gesetzt werden können, dass Gesetzentwürfe, die sie nicht schnell annehmen lässt, durch Notverordnung erlassen werden.'

[4] Article 18, (3) and (4). Kelsen considers, however, that this last provision would not apply to ordinances passed during the period of ninety days during which it was legal for the President and Government to rule without Parliament. He admits, however, that 'die Verpflichtung der Regierung, eine von ihr erlassene Notverordnung dem Parlament unverzüglich vorzulegen, bedeutet eine wichtige Einschränkung dieses ausserparlamentarischen Gesetzgebungsrechtes'. (*Jahrbuch des öffentlichen Rechts*, vol. xviii, p. 142.)

cases of necessity and for purposes of defence.[1] But, as Kelsen points out, this safeguard was worthless from a legal point of view.[2]

The President was also made head of the army.[3] But this was rather a change of emphasis than an actual increase in presidential power. It may be noted, however, that the reforms gave more power to the army. Hitherto it had only been empowered to restore order if so requested by the civil powers. It was now permitted to step in, in case of emergency, without being so requested.[4]

Another marked tendency in the 1929 reforms was towards centralization. But although it was coming to be realized with increasing clearness in responsible circles that Austria could not afford the luxury of provincialism—either from a moral or from an economic standpoint—yet as Kelsen had pointed out two years earlier, this tendency was, if anything, gaining ground,[5] in spite of the increased centralization introduced by the 1925 reforms, and in spite of the general realization that provincialism must make the possibility of an *Anschluss* ever more remote.

It was also intended to introduce changes as regards the organization of the Upper House, which, it was generally admitted, had not worked satisfactorily.[6] The *Heimwehr*, the *Landbund*,[7] and certain other right-wing sections of Christian Socialist opinion were anxious to introduce the corporative principle, either wholly or in part. And a proposal was for a time considered by which the nine Provinces were to be repre-

[1] Article 18, (3).

[2] 'Da das Vorhandensein dieser Umstände zu beurteilen, dem Ermessen der verordnenden Instanz selbst überlassen bleibt, und dieses Ermessen auch von dem seiner Überprüfung zuständigen Gericht—dem Verfassungsgerichtshof—nicht wirksam überprüft werden kann.' (Op. cit., p. 141.)

[3] Article 80, (1).

[4] Article 79, (2).

[5] 'Durch die politische u. staatsrechtliche Entwickelung seit dem Umsturz hat sich die Stellung der Länder so gekräftigt, haben sich die durch die Landesregierungen repräsentierten politischen Machtcentren in den ehemaligen österreichischen Krönlandern so sehr verwurzelt, dass an eine Umwandlung Österreichs in einen Einheitsstaat ernstlich nicht mehr zu denken ist.' (*Frankfurter Zeitung*, 4 April 1927.)

[6] Seipel, article in *Reichspost*, 19 October 1929.

[7] *Die Stunde*, 21 September 1929.

sented by eighteen members, while thirty-six members should represent the professions and industries.[1] However, as Schober pointed out, a reform of such magnitude could not be hurried through in a few days—particularly as it would mean a further increase in the number of officials.[2] It was anticipated, however, that another constitutional law would be passed dealing with this matter. In the meantime the composition of the Federal Council remained unchanged.[3]

A further step towards centralization was taken by extending the control of the Court of Audit not only over provincial finances but over districts which comprised more than twenty thousand inhabitants.[4] Hitherto the control of the Court of Audit had only been exercised in those Provinces which had not independent control organs of their own.[5] This change brought the finances of the city of Vienna under the control of the Court of Audit, and in consequence was bitterly opposed by the Social Democrats.

The right of appeal in matters dealing with provincial administration was somewhat extended.

The powers of the State police were considerably extended at the expense of those of the Provinces.[6] As a result of this legislation, the special municipal police force instituted in Vienna after the 1927 riots had to be disbanded. All State police were to be given an autonomous ordinance right, in virtue of which they could, under special circumstances, issue ordinances, which would have temporary validity, provided

[1] *The Times*, 15 October 1929. [2] *Reichspost*, 20 October 1929.

[3] But although no new legislation was introduced, a later paragraph referred to members of the Upper House as enjoying immunity in their capacity as members of Provincial Councils (Article 58, (1)). But the old Federal Council members, although they had to be eligible for election, could not themselves be members of local assemblies (Article 35, (2), 1920).

[4] Smaller districts could be included if the Provincial Government concerned so requested (Article 127).

[5] B. G. Bl. Nr. 268, 30 July 1925, Article 127, (1).

[6] Kelsen, *Jahrbuch des öffentlichen Rechts*, vol. xviii, p. 132. 'So gut wie die gesamte Sicherheitspolizei ist der Zuständigkeit der Länder entzogen, und dem Bunde übertragen. Diese Monopolisierung fast des gesamten Polizeiwesens beim Bund bedeutet, wenn man beachtet, dass auch das ganze Militärwesen u. die ganze Gerichtsbarkeit von allem Anfang an beim Bund lagen—einen Grad von Zentralisation, der mit dem Typus des Bundesstaates kaum mehr vereinbar ist.'

that they did not contravene existing laws.[1] Schober gave an assurance that this legislation was only intended to endow the police with such additional facilities for keeping order as no law-abiding man could take exception to.

The State Minister for Education was now given control over all matters concerning education[2]—a concession on the part of the Social Democrats.

The future position of Vienna was the subject of much bitter controversy. The Christian Socialists, seeing in its independence the key to many of the evils of post-war Austria, wished to deprive it of its provincial status, and reduce it to the position of a federal city under the direct control of the Federal Government. They maintained that it was not that Vienna was of lesser importance than the other Provinces, but that she was essentially different from them.[3] Her independent position as a Province could not, in their opinion, be reconciled with her special obligations as the capital city of the whole of Austria.[4] This, however, seemed to the Social Democrats like an attempt to have things both ways—federalism and the abolition of Viennese autonomy. But the Christian Socialists pointed out, with some truth, that the position of the Mayor of Vienna was very much stronger than that of an ordinary provincial Governor.[5] The Social Democrats argued, however, that it was ludicrous that the mayor of a city comprising two million persons should be reduced to the status of a mere *Bezirkshauptmann*, while a tiny province like Vorarlberg, comprising only 140,000 persons, should be in a position of

[1] Kelsen comments as follows on these provisions: 'Mit der Vorschrift, dass die von den Polizeibehörden zu erlassenden Verordnungen, nicht gegen bestehende Gesetze verstossen dürfen, stellt sich die Verfassung auf den Standpunkt der mehr als fragwürdigen Lehre, die zwischen Verordnungen secundum Legem, praeter Legem u. contra Legem unterscheidet.' (Op. cit., p. 143.)

[2] Article 120, (1); *Frankfurter Zeitung*, 5 December 1929.

[3] *Reichspost*, 12 October 1929.

[4] 'Der geschichtlich gewordene, legitime Länderföderalismus ist ein Wesen für sich, u. kann nicht verwechselt werden mit der Stellung der Bundeshauptstadt, die als solche besondere Verflichtungen gegenüber dem ganzen Bund, als Sitz aller zentralen Institute hat.' (*Reichspost*, 19 October 1929.)

[5] *Reichspost*, 19 October 1929.

comparative independence.[1] According to the original proposals put forward by Schober in the form of three Bills, on 18 October, Vienna was deprived of its provincial status, and made directly dependent on the Federal Government. The powers of the Mayor were transferred to a Cabinet Minister, and the City Council reduced to twelve members.[2] These proposals could not, however, be carried, as the status of Vienna was an issue over which the Social Democrats were prepared to fight. And, in the end, Vienna retained its status as a Province. But a part of its revenue was in the future to be handed over to Lower Austria,[3] and a certain measure of control was accorded to the Federal Government regarding police, finance, and educational matters. And it was now possible to appeal to the Federal Government against decisions of the Mayor.

It may be noted that no provision was made by the new reforms for the existence of a 'State of Emergency', although this contingency had been provided for in the Weimar Constitution.[4] Kelsen draws attention, however, to the new provision of Article 102.[5] The intention of this passage is, Kelsen thinks, obscure. It may merely mean that measures normally within the competence of the local authority may be temporarily taken over by federal officials. It is not, however, expressly stated that the federal officials can only undertake matters which would be within the competence of the local authorities. Kelsen thinks it may be interpreted to mean that federal officials can, in such circumstances, take any measures which they may consider necessary to restore order. In this case, the provisions of the article do not seem to differ

[1] *Vorarlberger Volksblatt*, 19 October 1929.

[2] *Daily Telegraph*, 19 October 1929

[3] The German Nationalists had wanted the amalgamation of Vienna with Lower Austria. (*Frankfurter Zeitung*, 24 October 1929.)

[4] Article 48. Kelsen comments on this fact: 'Durch die Notverordnungen gemäss Art. 18 kann jedenfalls kein verfassungsmässig gewährleistetes Recht aufgehoben werden.' (*Jahrbuch des öffentlichen Rechts*, vol. xviii, p. 144.)

[5] 'Ergibt sich in einzelnen Gemeinden die Notwendigkeit, wegen Gefährdung der öffentlichen Ruhe u. Ordnung, besondere Massnahmen zu treffen, so kann der zuständige Bundesminister mit diesen Massnahmen für die Dauer der Gefährdung eigene Bundesorgane betrauen.'

essentially from those of Article 48 of the Weimar Constitution.

In general, however, the reform when passed[1] did not institute any very revolutionary changes, nor was the passage of the Bill marked by any grave disturbances. The Social Democrats, who had at first opposed reform, in the end agreed to it, chiefly because they feared that resistance might result in a *Heimwehr Putsch.* They were, however, only prepared to agree to moderate measures, and made it clear that any attempt to push through an extremist programme without their consent (which was constitutionally necessary, as a two-thirds majority was required for passing measures affecting the constitution) would meet with unflinching resistance.[2] Their attitude was no doubt stiffened by promises of help from Germany.[3] But in the main, in spite of much provocation from the *Heimwehr*,[4] the party remained surprisingly calm. This was, no doubt, partly due to Schober's tactfulness, although in his negotiations with Herr Danneberg, the representative of the Social Demo-

[1] 18 October: Three bills presented to National Council. 23 October: After debate on first reading they were turned over to the Constitutional Committee. 28 October to 8 November: The Constitutional Committee delegated detailed discussion to a sub-committee of eight, of all parties. Negotiations between Schober and Danneberg completed on 13 November. 7 December: The bills voted by the National Council.

[2] Cf. Bauer's speech at the Congress of the League of Republican Defence: 'The time may come, and perhaps sooner than one thinks, when laws will be attacked, and we will defend them. The working class should be resolute in employing all its forces—life and death.' (*Le Temps*, 21 October 1929.)

Deutsch: 'We warn them that if an illegal situation arises in Austria, there will be civil war in the country, that is to say, the death of thousands of men, the destruction of property, the ruin of the national economy, and the loss of the Austrian people.'

[3] Cf. speech of Herr Hoeltermann, delegate of the *Reichsbanner*, at the Congress of the League of Republican Defence: 'There are hundreds of thousands of workmen in Germany prepared to defend democracy in Austria. If you need our support we stand ready to help you.' (*The Times*, 22 October 1930.)

[4] e.g. a pamphlet issued by Steidle and Pfrimer on 18 October: 'The once proud Socialists, driven into a corner, must bow their heads though boiling with fury. Herr Schober has got all that it is possible to get out of democracy and parliamentarism, and we accept it as the first payment on account for the *Heimwehr* idea, but that does not end our fight. It merely consolidates our ground before advancing.' (*Daily Telegraph*, 19 October 1929.)

crats, he was considerably hampered by the attitude of the right wing of his own party.[1]

However, most of the more controversial measures were, in the end, abandoned. The position of Vienna remained substantially unchanged. The right of the executive to issue ordinances without authority from the legislature was restricted. The proposal to make constitutional a future change of the constitution by a simple majority was withdrawn.[2] Trial by jury, which it had been proposed to abolish in certain cases, was maintained. It may be said that the essentials of democratic government were maintained.[3] But it was clear that the emphasis on the new reforms was no longer, as before, on the safeguarding of the democratic principle.[4] The voting age was raised from twenty to twenty-one. The age of eligibility for election was raised from twenty-

[1] *Daily Telegraph*, loc. cit.: 'The *Heimwehr* will see to it that the wretched compromising weaklings in the bourgeois camp are swept away in a storm of popular fury if they attempt to realize their cherished desire of reaching an agreement with the Socialists.'

[2] This had occasioned great excitement in opposition circles; see comment of *Frankfurter Zeitung*, 19 October 1929: 'Die einfache Mehrheit könnte also z. B. die Einführung der Monarchie beschliessen. Hier zeigt sich der Charakter dieser Novelle als Vorstufe zu weiteren Änderungen.'

In view of later events, it is interesting to note a suggestion which appeared in an article in the *Reichspost* on 8 October: 'Ist zur Verfassungsänderung die Zustimmung des Nationalrates erforderlich? "Nein" sagt der Verfassungsgerichtshof.' The article went on to explain that in virtue of a law passed on 24 July 1917 (B. G. Bl. Nr. 307) the Government was empowered to take special measures, in case of a state of affairs brought about by the war, to safeguard the economic interests of the State. The present condition of affairs had been brought about by the war; and an alteration of the constitution was necessary in the economic interests of the State. A revision of the constitution could, therefore, be effected by the Government without consulting Parliament. It was noted in the *Reichspost* of 27 November that the Social Democrats were now agitating for the repeal of this war-time measure. The idea was ridiculed, but three and a half years later Dollfuss succeeded in dissolving Parliament for the last time, in virtue of its authority.

[3] This was partly a consequence of the fact that by 11 November the partial results of the municipal elections had not turned out favourably for the *Heimwehr*, who therefore feared that if they forced a general election the results might not be favourable to them. (*Daily Telegraph*, 11 November 1929.)

[4] For instance, the phrase 'vom ganzen Bundesvolk gewählt' was no longer a part of Article 1.

four to twenty-nine. Immunity rights were restricted.[1] Voting was made compulsory.[2]

These were merely signs, showing which way the wind was blowing. But the *Heimwehr* and the right-wing Christian Socialists openly asserted that the reforms could only be regarded as preliminary to greater changes.[3] And *The Times* of 9 December 1929 quoted a *Heimwehr* manifesto as follows: "It is not possible to regard the results obtained as the final realization of our aims, but simply as the first step of our movement towards the final end."[4]

[1] *Germania*, 21 October 1929. [2] Article 19.

[3] The *Frankfurter Zeitung* of 7 December quotes the *Reichspost* as remarking: 'Durch den hartnäckigen Widerstand der Sozialdemokraten sei nämlich die bessere ursprüngliche Verfassungsvorlage vereitelt worden, u. die neue Vorlage bedeute keinen Abschluss sondern nur eine Etappe auf dem Wege zur vollen Reform, den weiter zu gehen, die Staatsinteressen erforderten.'

[4] For text and general discussion of the significance of the 1929 reforms, see *Jahrbuch des öffentlichen Rechts*, vol. xviii; Kelsen, *Die Verfassung Österreichs*, pp. 130–60.

V

THE INFLUENCE OF THE PARTY SYSTEM ON THE EVOLUTION OF DEMOCRATIC GOVERNMENT

PARLIAMENTARY democracy, as a form of government, can only be successful when the parties are more or less at one in their fundamental aims, and are ready to compromise as to the methods best calculated to attain them. An attempt should therefore be made to estimate how far divergences in the political theories of the various parties in the State contributed towards bringing about the breakdown.

It is undeniable that there was an absolute divergence between the political theories of the more extreme exponents of Austro-Marxism and that of the right-wing Christian Socialists, and that no satisfactory compromise between the two creeds would have been possible.

The aim of the Austro-Marxists from 1919 on was the supersession of the capitalist-bourgeois State by a socialist proletarian one.[1] Most of the leaders, however, believed that this aim could only be achieved if Austria were joined on to Germany, because 'independence' meant that the Allies could starve her out if they disapproved of her policy; the realization of the *Anschluss* was, therefore, the first point of their programme. It is true that hatred of the Bolsheviks was always a marked characteristic of the Austrian Social Democrats. But this animosity was occasioned rather by a dislike of Bolshevik methods than by disapproval of Bolshevik aims.[2] And it was

[1] Bauer, 'Die alte u. die neue Linke', *Kampf*, July 1920: 'Die Eroberung der Demokratie stellte uns daher vor die Frage, in welche Weise u. mit welchen Mitteln wir auf dem neu eroberten Terrain den Kampf um den Sozialismus zu führen haben.' See also the Linz Programme of the Social Democratic Party, 1926. One of the points incorporated in this programme was: '. . . die überwindung der kapitalistischen, der Aufbau der sozialistischen Gesellschaftsordnung'.

[2] '. . . nicht der Kommunismus das trennende Moment, sondern der Bolshevismus, nicht also die prinzipielle Grundlage, sondern bloss die Taktik.' (Max Adler, 'Sozialismus u. Kommunismus,' January 1919, *Kampf*: Cf. *Kampf*, July 1921, article by Max Adler.) '. . . Im Willen zum Sozialismus ist die Arbeiterklasse einig. Nur um den Weg zum Ziele ist Streit.' (*Arbeiter Zeitung*, 15 March 1919.)

stated, over and over again, unequivocally, by the party leaders, in the party press, and at party conferences from 1919 to 1934, that the aim of the Social Democrats was the establishment of a purely socialist republic, from which bourgeois influence would be entirely eliminated; although it was generally admitted that a policy of conciliation was temporarily necessary. No permanent agreement between the two classes was, however, considered either possible or desirable.[1]

For the right-wing leaders of the Christian Socialists also, parliamentary democracy was regarded as a temporary form of government. Co-operation with the Social Democrats was felt to be a necessary evil in the immediate post-war period. But in time, it was hoped, socialist wings might again be clipped, and a return made to some form of autocratic government.

This essential divergence in aim of the extremist wings was widened by the personal antagonism between the leading exponents of both creeds. Monsignor Seipel, for instance, necessarily always a Catholic first and an Austrian afterwards, thought that the triumph of the Social Democrats would mean the end of Catholicism in Austria. He saw, in Otto Bauer, the foe *par excellence* of his Church. Bauer, on the other hand, argued that Seipel had deliberately chosen to use the Church as a pawn in his political game.[2] He maintained that, if the

[1] *Arbeiter Zeitung*, 5 January 1919: '. . . die politische Revolution ist nur die halbe Revolution. Sie hebt die politische Unterdrückung auf, aber sie lässt die wirtschaftliche Ausbeutung bestehen. . . . Haben wir dazu die Allgewalt des Kaisers gestürzt, um der Allgewalt des Kapitals unterworfen zu bleiben.'

See also Linz Programme (op. cit.), 1926: 'Eine solche Kooperation der Klassen' (as in a parliamentary democracy like Austria) 'kann . . . nur eine vorübergehende Entwicklungsphase in Klassenkampf um die Staatemacht, aber nicht das Ziel dieses Kampfes sein.'

Julius Braunthal, 'Moskau oder Paris?', *Kampf*, October 1920: 'Wer die Koalitionspolitik der Österreichischen Sozialdemokratie unter einem anderen Gesichtspunkt als dem der Abwehr der Konterrevolution betrachtet, hat sie nie begriffen.'

Deutsch, 'Der Geist der Revolution', *Kampf*, 4 October 1919: 'Die Koalition ist solange keine Gefahr solange wir geistig frei bleiben, u. uns nicht auf die schiefe Bahn einer Klassen-harmonie drängen lassen.'

[2] Bauer, *Sozialdemocratie, Religion u. Kirche* (Wien, 1927): 'Der Klericalismus macht die Religion zur Parteisache der Partei der Bourgeoisie, um auf die Religion der Volksmassen, die Herrschaft der Bourgeoisie zu stützen.'

interests of the Church were to be identified with those of the Christian Socialist party, if it became one of the main planks of the Christian Socialist platform, then the Social Democrats had no option but to fight it. The Church should be removed entirely from the arena of party politics.

It must be stated, however, in fairness to Seipel, that the cry of 'Religion ist Privatsache' was almost certainly only the thin end of the wedge, for the fact that the leaders of the Social Democrats were, for the most part, not only anti-clerical but also anti-Christian can hardly be contested. Most of them thought, however, that religion should not be actively attacked as it had been in the *Aufklärung* period. With the improvement in economic conditions which they anticipated from socialist administration, religion would, in any case, they thought, die a natural death.[1] In this, as in other cases, the Social Democrat leaders hoped to achieve their aims by peaceful, gradual methods. Bauer deprecated even the intellectual violence of the Free Thinkers. But the personal struggle between Bauer and Seipel was so fierce as to preclude the possibility of peaceful development in any direction. Every small issue which arose was turned by them into party capital.

On the Social Democrat side, the ascendancy of the left wing, represented by such men as Bauer, Deutsch, and Adler, was in part a consequence of the fact that they were intellectually very much abler than the more moderate leaders, such as Renner, Ellenbogen, and Leuthner. They were thus able to exert an influence on the policy of the party which was probably out of proportion to the extent of their following among the rank and file of the members.[2] This influence was, however, almost

[1] Speech of Otto Bauer at the Linz Conference, op. cit., 1926. Also, Otto Bauer, *Sozialdemokratie, Religion u. Kirche*: 'Die Religion ist dem wissenschaftlichen Sozialismus nicht, wofür sie der Liberalismus hielt, blosser Pfaffentrug, der durch blosse Aufklärung überwunden werden könne, sondern das Spiegelbild der wirtschaftlichen u. sozialen Lebensbedingungen der Menschen.'

[2] On the other hand, there existed a revolutionary group to the left of these leaders, for the pronouncedly left-wing view of the Social Democrats had prevented the revolutionaries from joining the Communists in any number. The fact that potentially Communist elements found their spiritual home among the Social Democrats explains in part the attacks made from time to time on the 'moderate' policy of the party.

always used to put a brake on the party when questions of practical politics arose.[1] Indeed, one of the most marked features of Austro-Marxism was its theoretical extremism and its practical moderation.

The adoption of this policy in the post-war period was largely due to the influence of Bauer, who considered that the future of Austro-Marxism depended upon the maintenance of the spirit of revolutionary fervour in the party on abstract questions of socialist doctrine, combined with a moderate policy on practical issues. Bauer hoped, by this policy, to retain within the party extreme left-wing elements, which would otherwise have drifted away towards communism, and to keep the end of the socialist society ever in view, while at the same time extending the influence of the party over the peasants and lesser bourgeoisie, by a practical policy of moderation. He saw clearly in the immediate post-war years that a policy of extremism would in practice lead to the intervention of the Allies, and the triumph, as in Hungary, of a counter-revolution. He emphasized over and over again the fact that conditions in Austria were entirely different from those in Russia, where the peasants had been willing, at first, to co-operate with the revolutionaries, because of their desire for land. It was this co-operation alone which had made the Bolshevik revolution feasible. In Austria, however, no co-operation would be forthcoming from the peasants, who had long been firmly established as landholders. Revolution was not, therefore, immediately feasible.

Bauer's policy was not, however, an entirely opportunist one, for he firmly believed that the future of socialism depended as much on the intellectual development of the workers as on their conquest of material power, and for this reason also he was not averse to a policy of gradualness.[2] On the other hand, he came to fear, after the Vienna riots of 1927, that the peaceful

[1] Both in 1927 and in 1934 the left-wing leaders were forced into action against their will, by uncontrollable extremist agitators.

[2] Bauer's speech at the Linz Conference, 1926: '... Ihr Sieg nicht nur davon abhängt, dass sie die Macht erobert, sondern auch davon, dass sie in sich selbst jene moralischen u. intellektuellen Qualitäten entwickelt, ohne die der Sozialismus nicht aufgebaut werden kann.'

development which he honestly desired might be made impossible by the activities of the right-wing extremists. He saw that the nearer the party came to victory by peaceful constitutional means the more the right-wing Christian Socialists would come to rely on force for its suppression.[1] If the Social Democrats, having lost control of the army, did not defend themselves against this threat, they would probably have to submit to forcible liquidation by the fascists. If, on the other hand, they developed an armed force, they would almost certainly be beaten if it came to an open fight with the Christian Socialists, who would have control over the army and the police force, as well as the *Heimwehr* and the other armed bodies of the right. Moreover, Bauer realized that any signs of militancy on the part of the Social Democrats would react unfavourably on their position *vis-à-vis* their more moderate followers.

On the whole, the Social Democrats, confronted by this dilemma, followed the second course. But the riddle was never wholly resolved, and Bauer himself pursued an uncertain course after 1927. However, he continued, as a rule, to urge moderation on the party, and, in particular, to try to reach some agreement with the other parties as regards disarmament, for he knew that, in the last resort, the Social Democrats could never be as strong as their rivals in this respect. It is probable, however, that apart from this consideration he had a genuine aversion to the idea of physical force.[2] All his violence was of the mind. He was not, however, as Renner and Ellenbogen, on the whole in favour of a coalition, even in 1931, when the danger of the position had become apparent. But he continued

[1] Speech at the Party Conference in 1927.

[2] Speech at the Party Conference in 1926: 'Was klug ist, das sollte man dieser Generation nicht mehr erzählen mussen . . . Bürgerkrieg, das heisst also, dass der Sozialismus, selbst im Falle des Sieges für eine ganze Generation keine Verbesserung der wirtschaftlichen Lage der Arbeiter bringen kann, sondern eine Verschlechterung bringen muss, weil die Zerstörung des Wirtschaftslebens unvergleichlich mehr ausmacht als die Konfiscation des Mehrwertes.' He was also aware of the inevitable danger of the use of force: 'Wer zur Gewalt greift, der ist der Gefangene der Gewalt.' On the other hand, at the Party Conference in 1929, he expressed the view that the only way to force disarmament on the other side was to arm so effectively as to terrorize the bourgeoisie into acquiescence.

to plead for strict discipline within the party, for he feared that in the last resort the decision would not rest with the Social Democrats but with the interested powers outside Austria, who would intervene in support of the bourgeois groups if it came to an actual test of strength.[1]

It became, however, increasingly difficult to combine revolutionary theory with practical moderation and, from the spring of 1933, it was apparent that the leaders of the Social Democrats were no longer in a position to control the party to whom they had preached revolution for so long.

Another reason for the ascendancy of left-wing elements among the Social Democrats was the fact that almost all the party officials, as well as the leaders, were Jews. The Jewish tendency towards extremism thus accentuated the natural tilt of the party towards the left.

Almost precisely the same forces were at work on the Christian Socialist side. Here also the ablest men were the extremists. Monsignor Seipel, as Bauer, stood head and shoulders above any of his colleagues. He shared with Bauer a belief in general principles, and a tenacity in fighting for what he believed to be right, not often found among Austrian public men. And he succeeded in inspiring Catholic policy in Austria with a fighting spirit hitherto unknown. The price which had to be paid for the rebirth of this more forceful form of political Catholicism was the alliance of the Church with the big Vienna bourgeoisie, who, far more than the Christian Socialist peasants of the Provinces, shared Seipel's hatred of the Social Democrats. Seipel was, however, undoubtedly a very great and very able man. Similarly, to take a few outstanding examples, Vaugoin, who reorganized the army after the war, Funder, the editor of the *Reichspost*, and Mataja, all men of pronouncedly right-wing views, were very much abler than Kunschak, the moderate leader of the Viennese Christian Socialists, or Hemala, the leader of the Christian Trade Unions, or the peasant leader, Reither. And it was the extreme elements who had capital behind them, in shape of support from the big Jewish industrialists.

[1] Speech at the Party Conference of 1931.

On the other hand, it is certainly true that there were large moderate groups in both camps, who would probably have been ready to work together permanently, within the framework of a democratic parliamentary régime, had the opportunity offered. Men like Renner, for instance, from the beginning explicitly repudiated any connections with communism.[1] And Austerlitz, the left-wing editor of the *Arbeiter Zeitung* and a man of great influence in the party, protested strongly, in 1926, against the tendency of the left-wing leaders to play with the idea of a dictatorship as being the only means of achieving their aims.[2] He said that he considered it nonsense to talk of the 'dictatorship' of the bourgeoisie since the war.

The views of these moderate elements did undoubtedly have a very considerable influence over the policy of the party, and, as has been pointed out, even the extremists for the most part subscribed to them as a temporary expedient when the unrest in the country began to assume really serious proportions. Thus, in 1929, the party put forward a strong plea for the disbandment of all private armed forces and for moderation.[3] It is probable, of course, that many of the men who advocated the adoption of this policy of co-operation and moderation believed, like Seitz,[4] Bauer, and Austerlitz, that it was only the means to the end, which was the triumph of the proletarian revolution. But it is also probable that many of those who paid lip-service to the revolutionary ideal were, at heart, far from averse to a permanent co-operation with their rivals. —Men like Renner, for instance, who refused even to pay lip-service,[5] advocated not only disarmament, but also the forma-

[1] Speech at the Linz Conference, 1926.

[2] Speech at the Linz Conference, 1926: 'Wenn der Parteitag zu erkennen gäbe, dass er die Demokratie geringschätzt, dass er in ihr keine wesentliche Errungenschaft wahrnimmt, so würde das sicherlich auch zu einer Minderung unserer Anziehungskraft auf die breite Masse führen.'

[3] Report of 1929 Party Conference: 'Der Parteitag betrachtet die vollständige innere Abrüstung, die restlose Auflösung aller Wehrformationen als das wirksamste Mittel, die friedliche, demokratische Entwickelung der Volkswirtschaft u. den stetigen Aufstieg der Arbeiterklasse sicherzustellen.'

[4] Speech at the 1930 Party Conference: 'Wir wollen keinen Krieg . . . wir wollen Frieden u. Arbeit. Wir werden mithelfen, wenn ihr sie wollt.'

[5] Speech at the 1927 Party Conference: '. . . es ist eine Gefahr u. ein Widerspruch, immer von Revolutionen zu reden, u. zugleich behaupten zu müssen, dass man sie nicht machen könne.'

tion of a coalition with the moderate bourgeois groups. He was acutely conscious of the dangers of the situation after 1927, when the tempo of rearmament was increasing rapidly on both sides.[1] He pointed out at the Party Conference of 1930 that the elections had shown the existence of a large democratic majority of moderate views, and the dislike of the people for the extremist groups. This democratic majority should group itself round the Social Democrats.[2] Renner did not advocate a lasting alliance with any of the bourgeois groups, but he thought that the party should agree to temporary co-operation with those who stood for democratic principles. He was more conscious than any of the other party leaders at that time of the dangers implicit in the Nazi movement.[3] He was, however, too right-wing in his views for the party as a whole, and was never in a really influential position. Bauer, however, was, by 1930, also well aware of the dangers of intransigent opposition.[4] In fact, the chances for the triumph of a policy of co-operation might appear to have been considerable round about 1930.

[1] Speech at the Party Conference of 1927: 'Rüstung u. Gegenrüstung erzeugen eine Kriegspsychose unter den Bürgern desselben Staates, die es dahin bringen kann, dass nur einmal irgendwo zufällig ein Gewehr losgeht, und der Bürgerkrieg ist da.'

[2] Renner at Party Conference, 1930: 'Diese demokratisch fühlende Mehrheit sieht in uns ihr Zentrum u. ihre Führung, an sie schliessen sich Schober Block u. Landbund an, an sie lehnt sich der demokratisch denkende Flügel der Christlichsozialen an. Das wäre ja immer als die Zweidrittelmehrheit im Parlament. Warum bildet diese Zweidrittelmehrheit nicht eine Regierung.'

[3] Speech at the 1930 Party Conference: 'Der eigentlich gefährliche Gegner, der noch nicht da ist . . . ist der Nationalsozialismus. Und dieser Nationalsozialismus ist es deshalb, weil er vom Sozialismus die Ausserlichkeiten, die äussere Form u. gewisse Einzelheiten herausnimmt u. aufpflanzt auf den reaktionären Boden wirtschaftlich verzweifelten Menschen, der es ihnen möglich macht, zugleich die grimmigsten Feinde der Arbeiterklasse, die grimmigsten Feinde des Sozialismus zu sein, u. sich doch Sozialisten zu nennen.'

[4] Speech at Party Conference, 1930: 'Unsere Aufgabe muss sein zu verhindern, dass der Fascismus wieder in die Regierung komme. Wir müssen daher die gegenwärtige Regierung, obwohl es nicht unsere Regierung ist, obwohl es eine bürgerliche Regierung ist, obwohl Reaktionäre in ihr sitzen, trotzdem zu stützen versuchen, damit der Kurs nicht wieder nach rechts wieder in die Richtung Vaugoin—Stahremberg zurückfällt.'

Other developments, however, combined to play into the hands of the extreme elements on both sides. Economic conditions, for instance, contributed towards the growth of revolutionary tendencies, and the desire for desperate remedies, among the working classes; while among the propertied classes, increases in taxation, especially those imposed by the Vienna Socialist municipality, sharpened aristocratic yearnings for a return to pre-war conditions.

The control exercised by foreign Powers over Austrian economic and foreign policy also served to bring the whole system of parliamentary democracy into disrepute. This form of government was, as has been pointed out, in any case regarded by the extreme groups on both sides as a temporary expedient, and such an attitude grew more and more prevalent when it became apparent that parliamentary democracy was nothing more than a façade behind which Austria's foreign creditors worked their will. Again, economic conditions sharpened the already existing antagonism between the Provinces and Vienna. And, because economic necessity made imperative a modification of the federal structure of Austria, the hostility of the conservative peasants and land-owning classes forced into closer relationship with Vienna found partial expression in movements like the *Heimwehr*. The history of Austria from 1927 till 1934 is the story of force feeding upon force. Both antagonists armed because their rivals did so, although the moderates on both sides were willing to disarm if the other party would do so first.

The turning-point came with the splitting-up of the *Bürgerblock* in the 1930 elections, for with the defection of the Schober group the main body of the party was compelled to turn to extreme right-wing elements for support in its struggle against the Social Democrats. The anti-socialist front tended to split up more and more as time went on, for, after the failure of the attempted *Anschluss* in 1931, the German Nationalists began to drift right away into the Nazi camp, leaving their erstwhile allies with no alternative to the *Heimwehr*. Thus the divisions in Christian Socialist ranks, though they gave temporary encouragement to the Social Democrats, were in reality the beginning of the end, for reliance on the *Heimwehr* led almost inevitably to the crushing of the Social Democrats in 1934.[1]

The victory of the extremists was also in part a consequence of the tendency of both sides towards what may be described as party totalitarianism. This was especially the case on the Social Democrat side, for the tendency of the *Bürgerblock* to split up into small groups prevented this principle from working out so fully in their case. The Social Democrats, however, had from the beginning laid particular emphasis on the need for presenting a united front to the outside world, and had, indeed, been conspicuously successful in doing so.[2] They tried, with this end in view, to prevent the members of the party from coming into contact with people of other opinions who might influence them and draw them away from the Party orbit.[3] They therefore laboured to build up Social Democrat societies which would cover all a member's activities from the cradle to the grave. His intellectual and physical needs were all catered for within the party. The party provided him with his flat; built kindergartens for his children, organized sport clubs, literary clubs, political clubs, and social clubs for himself and his wife; took charge of his economic life, negotiating on his behalf with his bourgeois employers; and even provided burial clubs for his death. The organization of the Social

[1] It is interesting to note that Renner had drawn the attention of the party to this danger as early as 1929. He had urged that the Social Democrats should not make things too difficult for their opponents. 'Wir müssen mit unserem Bürgertum manchmal Geduld haben, auch in der Heimwehrsache.' (Speech at the 1924 Party Conference.) In 1930 he again drew attention, at the Party Conference, to this danger; although Seitz, on this occasion, spoke cheerfully of the approaching triumph of the Social Democrats.

[2] *Arbeiter Zeitung*, 9 January 1919. 'Es ist für das Proletariat weniger gefährlich, wenn es vorübergehend einen falschen Weg, aber diesen Weg einig u. geschlossen geht, als wenn es sich im Streit um den richtigen Weg spaltet. . . . Hundertmal lieber einen falschen Weg einig gehen—denn Fehler kann man dann wieder korrigieren—als um des rechten Weges willen, uns spalten.' (Bauer, at Party Conference, 1927.)

[3] It was even laid down, at the Linz Conference in 1926, that no member of the party could, without permission, carry on work which meant his appearance in public life with people who were members of other parties.

Democratic party in Vienna[1] was as a state within a state. The members scarcely became acquainted with the real bourgeois standpoint because they had no opportunity of mixing in bourgeois society.

The *Bürgerblock* never succeeded in organizing themselves in this way to anything like the same extent, because the interests of their members were much less susceptible of amalgamation. It is true that the Social Democrats included both Communist and *petit bourgeoisie* elements and a certain proportion of peasant elements. But the interests of these groups were nothing like so divergent as those of, for instance, the peasants and the industrialists of the *Bürgerblock*, nor were they numerous enough or strong enough to exercise much influence within the party. None the less, the same tendency towards totalitarianism may be seen working out in sections of the *Bürgerblock*. The *Heimwehr*, for instance, made strenuous efforts to attract all the various groups into their orbit. Their avowed aim was the abolition of party government.[2] This policy was the subject of violent and bitter attack from the Social Democrats. But, in fact, the attitude of both sides was equally inimical to parliamentary democracy, the only difference being that the Social Democrats succeeded in uniting their party, while the *Heimwehr* split up theirs yet further.

It is easy to see that the extreme emphasis of the Social Democrats on party organization in effect nullified the proper working of the constitution just as much as the *Heimwehr* movement. For instance, although the constitution had provided specifically for the representation of all shades of opinion by detailed provisions for proportional representation, the Social Democrats deliberately aimed at the elimination of differences of opinion among the workers. In so doing, they not only prevented the normal working of the proportional representation system by transforming their party into a mili-

[1] Organization was naturally less complete in the Provinces, where the party was numerically very much weaker, 52 per cent. of the party members being Viennese. For the relative strength of the party in the different provinces, see the Party Protocol, 1925.

[2] See the Korneuberger Programme of 18 May 1930. (P. T. Lux, *La Leçon de l'Autriche, 1919–37*, p. 81.)

tant and educative rather than a representative group, they almost made impossible the working of any form of parliamentary democracy, which must depend, in the last analysis, upon the possibility of people altering their opinions, compromising now on one issue, now on another, and moving from party to party. A rigid division between two or more groups in a state must make the whole system unworkable because a temporary majority thus becomes a permanent one, and the minority is faced with the alternative of permanent exclusion from power, or revolution. Moreover, the elaborate party structure necessary for the building-up of this totalitarian system almost inevitably places an undesirable amount of power in the hands of the party organizers, who become the real rulers of the state. This certainly tended to be the case in Austria.

In spite, however, of the fact that the party organizations, which were controlled by the more extreme elements on both sides, tended to separate the people into exclusive groups, the divergence in interests and outlook between the peasants and the workers, who formed the main bulk of the population, may easily be overestimated. It is true that the peasants were, in an overwhelming majority, conservative in their outlook, if by conservatism is meant adherence to private property. And it is true that the Social Democrats wished to substitute state for private ownership. On the other hand, the majority of the Social Democratic leaders realized from the start that they would only be able to put their theories into practice very slowly, and with great care, as far as the peasantry were concerned. The fact that conditions in Austria were entirely different from those in Russia, where the peasants had been willing to co-operate with the revolutionaries, because of their desire for land, was fully grasped. In Austria, there were comparatively few big estates, and the peasantry, although not prosperous, had a long tradition of semi-independence behind them. Any attempt forcibly to expropriate their property would have been, it was well understood, foredoomed to failure. A policy of peaceful permeation was the only feasible one. For this reason wholesale expropriation of privately owned land at no time formed part of the Social Democrats' programme.[1]

On the other hand, the party was, from the beginning, acutely conscious of the necessity of extending its influence among the peasantry.[2] In 1925 an official agricultural programme was drawn up. This programme provided for the retention of peasant ownership, although the big estates were to be expropriated.[3] The Social Democrats hoped, however, by a lavish expenditure on agricultural colleges and institutes, to educate the peasantry gradually to more scientific methods of farming, which would probably, in the end, mean amalgamation of small holdings, and a greatly increased State control.[4]

The party laid great emphasis also on the need for improving the position of the smaller peasants who had suffered from the inclosure of common land[5] and the conditions of work of the hired labourers. These latter lived, as a rule, in the peasant houses—or rather, in the stables—and their standard of living

[1] Article in the *Arbeiter Zeitung*, 26 March 1919, 'Arbeiter u. Bauern'. Bauer's speech at the Party Conference, 1925: 'Nicht mit Gewaltakten, nicht mit Gesetzen, sondern mit einem organischen Anpassungsprozess an die sozialistische Umgebung wird sich die Bauernschaft in die neue sozialistische Gesellschaft eingliedern.'

Also Bauer, *Der Kampf um Wald u. Weide*, 1925. See speeches made at 1927 Party Conference, on agricultural policy.

[2] Bauer, 'Leitsätze zur Agrarpolitik', *Kampf*, July 1921: 'Jeder weitere Fortschritt der proletarischen Revolution setzt die Eroberung stärkerer Machtpositionen in den Dörfern u. auf den Gutshöfen voraus.'

[3] The policy had been put forward in the *Arbeiter Zeitung* as early as 10 January 1919: 'Der Sozialismus will das Ausbeutungseigentum überwinden, nicht das Arbeitseigentum. Der Grund u. Boden des Adels, der Kirche, u. der Kapitalisten soll vergesellschaftet werden; der Grund u. Boden des Bauern soll sein Privateigentum bleiben.'

[4] 'Über die Tatsache, dass von einer Expropriation der Bauernschaft keine Rede sein kann, war nie ein Zweifel.' (Bauer, Party Conference, 1925.)

On the other hand, in the Linz Programme of 1926, it was envisaged that if amalgamation of property was required in the public interest, and if it was impossible to get the parties concerned to agree to it, amalgamation might be forced upon them. However, it was again laid down that 'der Sozialismus bekämpft das Raubeigentum der Herrenklassen, nicht das Arbeitseigentum der Bauern'. The peasant would, in fact, be in a stronger position than ever, after the liquidation of his capitalist creditors.

[5] The *Kleinbauernverband* was founded in 1923, and held its first Party Conference in Vienna in 1925. Membership was strongest in Lower Austria (3,500) and Kärnten (1,330).

was extremely low. The Social Democrats regarded them with great interest, as a potentially socialist element in the population, and agitated constantly for the building of separate houses for them, and for better working conditions, etc.[1] In those Provinces where hired labour formed a considerable element in the working population, the Social Democrats made good headway, but it cannot be said that their agricultural programme on the whole met with any considerable measure of success.

On the other hand, although the peasants showed a lack of interest in the abuses of women's labour, the problem of alcohol, the fate of the hired labourer, and other questions which exercised the Social Democrats, they were by far the most staunch supporters of democratic government.[2]

The hostility of men like Dr. Ender to the Viennese socialists after the war was not so much based on dislike of their democratic proclivities as on opposition to their policy of centralization. The *Bauernbund*, led by Dr. Reither, frequently protested against the reactionary politics of the Christian Socialist party leaders. And although it is true that a considerable number joined the *Heimwehr*, and later a very much larger number the Nazis, it is probable that the rank and file of the Austrian peasantry remained to the end supporters of the democratic principle.

Again, although it is true that the peasantry were, on the whole, Catholic in outlook, while the workers had drifted away from the Church, and were for the most part indifferent, if not hostile, in their attitude towards it, this divergence must not be overestimated. The lower clergy, who worked among the peasants, were very much more democratic in their views than their ecclesiastical superiors. The overwhelming majority were themselves of peasant stock and tended, therefore, to share the outlook of their flocks.[3] There were indications in 1932, for instance, that many of them strongly disapproved of the attitude adopted by their superiors towards the *Heimwehr*.

[1] See Bauer's speech on the Agrarian Programme of the Social Democrats at the 1925 Party Conference.

[2] Tyrol and Vorarlberg, in particular, looked back proudly on a centuries-old tradition of self-government.

[3] The higher clergy were also, for the most part, men of humble origin, e.g. Monsignor Seipel, Cardinal Innitzer.

In any case, the extent of clerical influence among the peasantry can easily be overestimated. The Austrians were not prone to take their religious life too seriously; and attempts made by the Church to extend its influence outside purely religious matters were not regarded with approval.[1] Anti-clericalism had its roots far back in the past, and had antedated by many decades the challenge of the socialists and the emergence of the Nazi party.

But if the clericalism of the conservative peasantry can easily be overestimated, so can the anti-clericalism of the Social Democrats. It is true that the party were prepared to fight what may be termed 'political Catholicism' because this was considered to be a force dangerous to the party.[2] But the Free Thinkers, who were actively hostile to the Church, were very small in number, and were strongly discouraged in their activities by Bauer, Renner, and most of the other leaders.[3] And, while it is true that the rank and file of the party were passively hostile to the Church, or at least, indifferent to its claims, certain leaders, as Ellenbogen and Leuthner, stated unequivocally that they considered this a source of weakness rather than of strength, to the party, and were anxious to see a revival of religion in the ranks of the Social Democrats.[4]

[1] On 20 October 1931, for instance, the *Neue Freie Presse* drew attention to the big peasant meeting, 4,000 strong, which had taken place at S. Johann im Pongau, and remarked that the peasants had demonstrated 'nicht nur gegen die Regierung u. die Parteipolitik, sondern auch gegen die politisierenden Geistlichen'.

[2] See the report prepared by the party executive for the Party Conference at Linz in 1926: 'Die römische Kirche übt ihre grosse Macht über die Seelen der breiten Massen, die ihrer Klassenlage nach, zu der Arbeiterklasse gehören, dazu aus, um sie von der Teilnahme an dem Befreiungskampf der Arbeiterklasse fernzuhalten, u. diese Massen in der Gefolgschaft bürgerlicher Parteien zu erhalten. . . . Dadurch stützt die römische Kirche die Herrschaft der Bourgeoisie.'

[3] Speech by Renner at the 1925 Social Democratic Party Conference, when the whole question was discussed: 'Ich möchte aber das eine betonen: es ist auch in dem Staat nicht Sache der Sozialdemokratie Partei, Religion u. Kirche zu bekämpfen.'

[4] Speech by Leuthner at the 1926 Party Conference: 'Im tiefsten Grund entstehen Religionen aus dem eingebornen, ewigen, unsterblichen u. durch nichts zu unterdrückenden Drang des gesamten Menschheitsgeschlechtes nach Erklärung der letzten Ursachen der Dinge.' He registered a strong protest against the attempt of the Free Thinkers to make acceptance of their creed the *sine qua non* of socialism. Cf. with speech of Preis: 'Seine Apostel'

Otto Bauer,[1] a simple workman, organized a group within the party known as the 'Religious Socialists'. He succeeded in establishing some contacts with the more sympathetic of the clergy.[2] The hostility of the Church, however, prevented the movement from achieving any considerable success.[3]

The policy of the Church itself was not, however, at any rate for the first seven years of the Republic, as reactionary as is sometimes supposed. After the breakdown the Bishops professed unequivocally their loyalty to the Republican régime[4] and there seems no reason to question the sincerity of this declaration. In 1925 they issued a Pastoral Letter which showed marked sympathy with the claims of the working classes,[5] although they were not prepared to tolerate any compromise with the Social Democrats.[6]

After 1927, however, conditions changed for the worse in this, as in so many other respects. The episcopate had been aroused by the anti-clerical programme which had been decided on by the Social Democratic Party Conference at Linz in 1926 (in spite of protest from the moderate element

---

(Free Thinkers) 'haben an Intoleranz ungefähr dasselbe geleistet wie die Vertreter aller übrigen Religionen zusammen.' And Mentasti pointed out that opposition to alcohol and opposition to the churches meant opposition to the only forms of relaxation open to the peasants.

[1] Not to be confused with his famous namesake, one of the greatest of the Social Democrats.

[2] e.g. with Prof. Fliegler.

[3] It was condemned by the Bishops in 1930 (see Kungebung, *Des österreichischen Episkopates zur sozialen Frage*, January 1930.)

[4] See pronouncement made by Cardinal Piffl, 4 November 1918: 'Treue gegenüber der Republik.' Pastoral Letter of the Bishops and Archbishops, 23 January 1919, in defence of democracy. (Knoll, A. M., Von Seipel zu Dollfuss, 1934, pp. 44–7.)

[5] See Knoll, op. cit., pp. 48–59. 'Uber Politik, Volkswirtschaft u. Moral. Demokratie u. Neue Staatsform.' The letter inveighed against the evils of capitalism in the strongest terms, because of the lack of regard shown by its leaders for the natural rights of the workers, and their attempt to dominate public life. 'Bei Gott ist kein Unterschied zwischen der Seele der Fabrikarbeiters u. der Seele des Fabrikherrn.' In April 1926, further instructions were issued to priests, urging them to inveigh against the usurious exploitation of the workers.

[6] In April 1926, Roman Catholics were forbidden, except under special circumstances, to join Social Democratic Trade Unions, or to vote for Social Democrats. (Knoll, op. cit., p. 135, 'Instructio pro clero in re soziali'.)

in the party). And the fighting in Vienna in 1927, which, partly owing to the drastic measures taken to repress the rioters by Seipel's Government, resulted in thousands of people leaving the Church, and deflected episcopal policy decidedly to the right. Seipel, for his part, turned to the anti-working-class big industrialists for support against what he conceived to be the danger *par excellence*. The hostile attitude of the Church towards the Schober Block at the November elections of 1930 occasioned much scandal.[1]

It would, however, probably be a mistake to regard the Church as the villain of the piece even after 1927. It continued to evince great interest in social problems.[2] And although the higher clergy, and perhaps the majority of the lower clergy, regarded the *Heimwehr* movement with favour, as being a useful weapon for curbing socialist influence, they could not be very enthusiastic about a movement so deeply tinged with Nazi anti-clericalism.[3]

Although it is true that in the two main groups, the Social Democrats and the Christian Socialists, the balance of power tended to pass to the extreme wings, other important groups existed who were much more moderate in their outlook, and who stood unequivocally for democratic government. The *Landbund*, for instance, an organization supported chiefly by the more wealthy peasants led by Herr Winkler, inveighed constantly against the fascist proclivities of the Christian Socialists and the *Heimwehr*. Even in 1929, when it supported a reorganization of the state on a corporative basis, hoping thereby to secure a better representation of agricultural interests, its members emphasized the fact that the movement

[1] *Stellungnahme zu den österreichischen Nationalratswahlen*, 9 November 1930, 26 October 1930. (See Knoll, op. cit., pp. 167–77.)

[2] Lent Pastoral Letter, 1928, inveighing against low wages of women and bad housing. *Fasten Hirtenbrief der Erzbischöfe u. Bischöfe Österreichs*, 1928. (Knoll, op. cit., pp. 150–3.)

[3] In January 1930 a declaration was issued declaring that the Church could not consecrate the flags of political parties—'Politischen Vereinen ist mit Rücksicht auf die überparteiliche Stellung der Kirche die Weihe der Fahnen nicht zu bewilligen'.

See also the Lent Pastoral Letter, February 1932, issued by all the Bishops, warning the people against the Nazis.

wanted a genuine, democratic organization, not fascism of the Italian variety.[1]

The *Bauernbund* was another peasant organization strongly democratic in its views. It represented a different section of peasant opinion, and was distinguished from the *Landbund* chiefly by the fact that it was strongly clerical in tone, whereas the *Landbund* was anti-clerical. But it was, if anything, even more staunch to the democratic principle and, from 1929 on, protested frequently against the authoritarian leanings of its wealthier counterpart.[2] Most of the peasants were organized in one or other of these groups.

The Viennese counterpart of the *Bauernbund* was the *Freiheitsbund* of Herr Kunschak. This organization was much more decidedly democratic in outlook than either of the peasant organizations, and emphasized constantly the dangers of right-wing extremism.[3]

This movement was closely associated with the Christian Trade Union movement, led by Dr. Hemala. But it was in the nature of things difficult for a Christian Socialist workingmen's organization to offer attractions to the workers comparable with those of the very much larger and wealthier Social Democratic organization. The group was on the whole disliked by both parties, and never achieved a strong position. Herr Kunschak's reiterated warnings to the Christian Socialists for the most part fell on barren ground.

Finally, reference must be made to the Schober Block, which appeared in 1930 as a group of moderate bourgeois parties, united by opposition to the fascist proclivities of the *Heimwehr* and the Social Democrats.

From this brief analysis of the structure of opinion in Austria in the post-war years, it is clear that, although forces were at work which made the successful working out of democratic

[1] At a later stage, the *Landbund* lost many members to the Nazis. And the attitude of the whole group towards this question was somewhat equivocal.

[2] Some of the local *Bauernbund* groups, however, supported the *Heimwehr*, and it is not easy to discover what proportion of the peasants were behind them. It is probable that opinion was fluctuating a good deal between 1928 and 1932.

[3] The views of this group were represented in Herr Kunschak's paper, the *Weltblatt*, a pronouncedly democratic organ.

government difficult, its roots among the people were strong. And it is just possible that had the Nazi party not appeared on the scene, and forced the Christian Socialists into a position of dependence on the *Heimwehr*, some compromise with the Social Democrats might have been found possible. But the fact that the *Heimwehr*, the only element wealthy and strong enough to provide a defence against the Nazis, was in a position of financial dependence on the Italians, who were thus in a position to dictate their terms, made the destruction of the Social Democrats almost inevitable.

VI

THE INFLUENCE OF FOREIGN POLICY ON THE EVOLUTION OF DEMOCRATIC GOVERNMENT

THE difficulties experienced by Austria in the conduct of her foreign relations contributed, indirectly, to the general disillusionment with parliamentary democracy which came to be felt throughout the country. For it was all too obvious that the democratic theory of a policy inspired and controlled by the wishes of the people bore little or no resemblance to the facts of the case. Austria was, in fact, controlled by her creditors, who had over her, literally, the powers of life and death. And, since her foreign relations were matters of great moment to them, they did not hesitate to impose their own views on her Governments. These views were not shared by the great majority of Austrians. Thus it came about that successive cabinets, from 1919 till 1934, were obliged to pursue a foreign policy of which the electorate disapproved. This was the more unfortunate because foreign policy was a question of very great importance for post-war Austria, and the gradual realization that it was a matter over which public opinion could exercise no control did not enhance the value of democracy in the eyes of the Austrians.

The disillusionment began almost immediately after the war, when Austria was frustrated by France and the Allies in her plan for union with Germany.

The possibility of an independent existence for Austria had never been seriously envisaged by any section of Austrian opinion after the break-up of the Empire, although certain elements in the Christian Socialist party had viewed the prospect of an *Anschluss* with some misgiving. Almost the first official pronouncement of the new republican Government had been to the effect that German Austria was a part of the German Reich.[1] Representatives from German Austria

[1] Article 2 of the Declaration of 12 November 1918 (B. G. Bl. Nr. 5). It was arranged, however, that Austria should continue, for the time being, to be organized as a separate state.

attended the deliberations at Weimar on this assumption.[1] Bauer has stated that "our most important aim in the peace negotiations had to be the assertion of our right to unite with Germany'.

It seems probable that the Social Democrats were right in maintaining that the chief hope of survival for the young and somewhat frail plant of Austrian republicanism lay in the close connection of German Austria with the Reich. The Allies were, however, strongly opposed to any extension of German influence in the Danube basin, and Article 188 of the Treaty of St. Germain forbade an *Anschluss*, either immediately or in the future, without the consent of the League Council.[2] This article was, not unnaturally, felt to be extremely unjust, and strong protests were made against it, both in Germany and Austria.[3]

On the other hand, although it is almost certainly true that Austria and Germany would have joined up in the autumn of 1918 had they not been forcibly prevented by the Allies from doing so, it is equally true that public opinion, never unani-

[1] On 6 February 1919, a message of congratulation was sent from the Provisional National Assembly, to the Assembly at Weimar, in which it was stated that the Austrian body '. . . spricht die Hoffnung u. die Überzeugung aus dass . . . es der deutschösterreichischen Volksvertretung gelingen wird, das Band, das Gewalt im Jahre 1866 zerrissen hat, wieder zu knüpfen, die Einheit u. Freiheit des deutschen Volkes zu verwirklichen u. Deutschösterreich mit dem deutschen Mutterlande für alle Zeiten zu vereinigen.'

Provision was made in due course by Article 61 of the Weimar Constitution for the early inclusion of Austria in the Reich.

[2] M. Beneš has since stated that he and Masaryk had envisaged until as late as 1917 the incorporation of Austria in Germany. They thought that this solution would constrain the remaining small states of Central Europe to form a close political and economic bloc. These ideas were only abandoned when it was found that they met with opposition from Italy, France, England, and Russia—especially the two former. 'Being completely loyal to our friends in the war . . . we accepted their standpoint in this matter, and have remained faithful to it up to now.' (Speech of 21 March 1934, *Czechoslovak Sources and Documents*, p. 29.)

[3] 'Die Nationalversammlung erhebt vor aller Welt feierlich ihren Protest dagegen, dass der Friedensvertrag von S. Germain unter dem Vorwande, die Unabhängigkeit Deutschösterreichs zu schützen, dem deutschösterreichischen Volke sein Selbstbestimmungsrecht nimmt, ihm die Erfüllung seines Herzenswunsches, seine wirtschaftliche, kulturelle, u. politische Lebensnotwendigkeit, die Vereinigung mit dem deutschen Mutterlande, verweigert.'

mous in this matter, became less fervent in its support as the months passed. The monarchists and the big Austrian industrialists had never been in favour of an *Anschluss*; and, after the publication of the German Peace Terms on 7 May, the Austrian bourgeoisie shrank from identifying themselves with Germany, especially as France succeeded in creating the impression that Austria would get more favourable peace terms if she abandoned the *Anschluss* policy. It was also felt that if France were presented with a *fait accompli*, she might well incite the Yugoslavs and Czechs to occupy Austrian territory. Germany, for her part, feared the loss of further territory to France and Poland.[1] As time went on, however, these misgivings were forgotten, and only the injustice of the Allies' veto was remembered.

Austria's position in the immediate post-war period was not a happy one, for, frustrated in what she now believed to have been her unanimous desire to join Germany, there was no Power, democratic or otherwise, to whom she could turn for assistance. Hungary, denuded of two-thirds of her pre-war territory, was, if anything, in a rather more unsettled condition than Austria. And the two states, never on particularly friendly terms, were now divided by the incipient dispute over the Burgenland.[2]

There could be no question of the establishment of close relations with Czechoslovakia. It is true that in both countries democratic Governments were in power, and that the relationship between them was ostensibly friendly. But Czechoslovakia was a victor state, who, having recouped herself lavishly at the expense of Austria, was not unnaturally anxious to sever all connections with her late rulers, even though these showed signs of an ideological change of heart. Moreover, disputes over the frontier had not yet died down.

If Austria's relationship with Czechoslovakia was distant, her relationship with Italy was, at this time, one of positive hostility, because of the question of the South Tyrol. In this

[1] Otto Bauer, *The Austrian Revolution*, Parsons (1925), p. 115.

[2] C. A. Macartney, *Hungary and Her Successors*, Oxford University Press (London, 1937), pp. 41 *et seq.*

case, as in the case of the veto on the *Anschluss* with Germany, the Austrians asserted bitterly that the principle of self-determination was only applied when the application was likely to work out in favour of the Allies.

Thus, in 1919, since there appeared to be no other alternative, German Austria had to subscribe to the policy of the Allies, and pose as an independent state. The maintenance of Austrian independence has been the official foreign policy of the country from the moment when Renner succeeded Bauer, the great protagonist of the *Anschluss*, on 28 July 1919.

Desirable though this policy may have been, from the point of view of Europe as a whole, it was an essentially artificial policy. And the fact that it had, for the most part, very little backing from public opinion, weakened considerably the standing in the country of the successive Governments who had to attempt to carry it out.

Opposition to official foreign policy amounted at times to a declaration of war on the Federal Government, and this at a time when national unity was a matter of prime importance.[1] These 'unofficial' agitations caused such grave disquiet in Allied, and particularly in French circles, that on 14 April 1920, M. Lefèvre Pontalis handed a Note to the Chancellor, on behalf of his Government, stating that, if the Austrian Government were not in a position to suppress the *Anschluss*

[1] In December 1919, Tyrol and Salzburg respectively petitioned to be allowed to join the Reich. On 31 March 1920 the Tyrol *Landtag* requested the Renner Government to present a petition to the Ambassadors' Conference for the union of Tyrol with Germany, on economic grounds. Renner replied that although he could not refuse to present such a petition, he deplored it. It would not be granted, and it would only have the effect of discrediting Austrian representatives in the eyes of the Allies and thus making negotiations for economic assistance more difficult. Tyrol, however, persisted: and Salzburg followed suit.

The difficulties of Renner's position were increased by the fact that he was not supported by his own party. On 5–7 November 1919, for instance, at the Social Democratic Party Conference, the party announced its continued adherence to a policy of *Anschluss*.

The same difficulties confronted the Christian Socialist Mayr cabinet, which came into office on 3 November 1919. On 3 February, for instance, a deputation from the Provinces demanded the organization of a plebiscite to decide whether or not an *Anschluss* petition should be presented to the League. Arrangements for such a plebiscite were made in Salzburg, on 11 March 1920 for 24 April; and in Steiermark on 7 April for 30 May.

agitations, the French Government would withdraw its support from schemes to help Austria. On hearing of this Note, the British and Italian Governments intimated to the Austrian Government that such an action on the part of France would mean the complete collapse of schemes to assist Austria. Thus the French Note really amounted to a command to the democratically elected Government of Austria to override and suppress the wishes of its electorate.[1]

In this way, the Austrian people were alienated in sympathy from their elected representatives, at the very time when it was most essential that the new state should be welded into a coherent whole, by leadership from a strong popular Government.

The goal of Austrian 'independence' was, moreover, receding rapidly into the distance. The conditions which it was felt necessary to attach to the granting of the League Loan in 1922 were such as to be scarcely compatible with the existence of Austria as an independent sovereign state at all.[2] League control was withdrawn in 1926. But it became all too obvious in 1931 that the narrow margin which had till then separated Austria from economic collapse would not suffice to enable her to stand up to the economic blizzard which descended upon Europe and America. And, in 1932, when the Lausanne Loan was granted, even more stringent League control was imposed.

It is true that by 1932 the situation had somewhat changed, for, with the rise of the Nazi movement in Germany, more moderate Austrian opinion came to regard a policy of indepen-

[1] The Note occasioned a stormy scene in the National Council in the course of which Mayr pointed out bluntly that Austria was not in a position to refuse the demands of the Allies: 'Wir werden ohne auswärtige Hilfe vielleicht schon in zwei Monaten nichts mehr zu essen haben.' (*Stenographische Protokolle*, 15 April 1920.)

Finally, the Mayr cabinet resigned on 1 June, on the grounds that the *Anschluss* agitations had made its position impossible.

[2] She had to agree to submit her finances, and the general economic policy of her Government, to control by a committee of the guarantors of the loan, which was to be represented in Vienna by a Commissioner-General. She had also to agree not to 'endanger' her independence by the granting of a 'special régime' to any one state. (League of Nations, *The Restoration of Austria*, Agreements arranged by the League of Nations and signed at Geneva on 4 October 1922, with the Relevant Documents and Public Statements. C. 716, M. 428, 1922, x, Geneva, 1922.)

dence with less disfavour. But the fact remains that for fourteen years, successive Austrian Governments were compelled to attempt to carry out a foreign policy which was directly contrary to the wishes of the great majority of the people by whom they had been elected. In fact, of course, the various Governments had no option in the matter; but an electorate frustrated in its dearest wish does not pause to consider the good reasons which may exist for this frustration, especially when its temper is sharpened by acute economic distress.

There can be little doubt that what the vast majority of the Austrian electorate wanted during these years was an *Anschluss* with Germany, although this desire was not always felt with equal intensity by the different sections of the population.[1]

The chief supporters of the *Anschluss* policy of 1919–22 had been the separatist peasantry of the Alpine province, who were influenced to a large extent by temporary economic considerations. After 1925 the movement derived its strength mainly from the Civil Service, the professional classes, and the industrialists. If less spontaneous, this later movement was very much better organized and, unlike its earlier counterpart, it received positive support from high places in Germany. It was the beginnings of the renascence of German nationalism.[2]

[1] In 1923 and 1924, for instance, agitations for an *Anschluss* died down, partly owing to the comparative success of the Reconstruction Scheme in Austria, partly because of the bad conditions then prevailing in Germany. After 1924, however, the agitations increased again, because, with the introduction of the Dawes Plan, conditions improved in Germany, at a time when they were deteriorating steadily in Austria, as a result of the collapse caused by the over-speculation which took place in the summer of 1924.

[2] *Le Temps*, 17 and 27 May 1925, and the *Deutsche Allgemeine Zeitung*, 26 May 1932.

The new German Nationalist movement may be said to have taken its inception from an unofficial visit paid by Dr. Dinghofer and Dr. Frank, the German Nationalist leaders, to Berlin, towards the end of January 1925. It was then decided to reorganize, on a wider basis, Professor Wettstein's committee, which had been formed in 1919, to work for the removal of the technical difficulties in the way of the *Anschluss*. The new organization, which met for the first time in Vienna on 26 February, designated itself the Austro-German Union, as the Social Democrats' Popular League had become merged in the new organization. Its members were from all parties. Various sub-committees were set up to consider such matters as the unification of teaching in the secondary schools of both countries (higher education

And large *Anschluss* demonstrations, attended by prominent officials, became increasingly frequent in both countries.[1] Yet, at the same time, Ramek and his Foreign Minister, Mataja, continued throughout the year to pursue a League policy, although his Government depended on the support of the very German Nationalists who were most opposed to this, and who were among the staunchest of the supporters of the Austro-German Union organization.

The one more or less constant desire of this feckless people could thus find no outlet through ordinary political channels. And, since this desire was too strong to be suppressed altogether, expression was given to it in extra-constitutional ways. The movement thus gained that momentum which so often comes to forces which are suppressed. And the methods used accustomed the Austrian people to reliance upon extra-constitutional means for attaining their ends. Thus, as the *Anschluss* movement gained in strength, so respect for ordinary parliamentary government decreased.

This curious and unsatisfactory situation occasioned much anxiety in France, Italy, and the countries of the Little Entente. But the sharp reactions of the interested Powers towards movements of opinion in Austria and Germany were bitterly resented in both countries. Dr. Mataja protested in May to a representative of *Le Matin* that the Powers appeared to have forgotten that they had themselves guaranteed Austrian 'independence'. It was, he pointed out, a grave psychological mistake to treat Austria as a pawn in the political game, to be bartered about to suit the convenience of Italy, France, and the Little Entente.[2]

As the work of *Ausgleichung* continued, however, it was found that the process of assimilation was not so easy as had been at

had already been unified), criminal law, agrarian reform on the German model, etc. It was hoped by these means to achieve a union *de facto* between the two countries, which would in time come to be recognized as a union *de jure*.

[1] See *Le Temps*, 6 May 1925, for an account of the Rhineland celebrations held in Vienna on 3 May.

[2] 'Ein Staat, der weder das Gefühl, noch den Stolz seiner Unabhängigkeit besitzt, kann sich nicht lange behaupten.' (Speech reported in the *Deutsche Allgemeine Zeitung*, 26 May 1925.)

first anticipated. It was, for instance, difficult to envisage any satisfactory solution for the problem of Austrian provincialism, were Austria to become incorporated in the Reich.[1] And it was found, on closer examination, that Austrian legislation did differ from German in many important respects.[2] Austrian industrialists were now not slow in pointing out that the structure of German industry was essentially different from that of Austrian.[3] Finally, the Social Democrats, once the most convinced of all the protagonists of the *Anschluss*, became ever more doubtful of the advisability of this policy, as the strength of the Nazi movement in Germany increased.[4]

The announcement of the Customs Union project by Curtius and Schober in March 1931 came therefore as something like a bombshell. But its reception by the great Powers indirectly knocked the last nail in the coffin of Austrian democracy, for, once the Customs Union had been forbidden, everybody became convinced that this was what they had

[1] Kelsen wrote in 1927: 'Durch die politische u. staatsrechtliche Entwicklung seit dem Umsturz hat sich die Stellung der Länder so gekräftigt, haben sich die durch die Länder-Regierungen repräsentierten politischen Machtzentren in den ehemaligen österreichischen Krönlandern so sehr verwurzelt, dass an eine Umwandlung Österreichs in einen Einheitsstaat ernstlich nicht mehr zu denken ist. Ja, man darf sich sogar—so traurig es ist—nicht verhehlen, dass wenn die Umwandlung Österreichs in einen Einheitsstaat... die Aufhebung der Länder also, eine conditio sine qua non für den Anschluss diese Bedingung nicht erfüllt werden könnte.' (*Frankfurter Zeitung*, 4 April 1927.)

[2] The German criminal code, for instance, was very much more severe than the Austrian. And German marriage laws were not easily reconcilable with Roman Catholic opinion in Austria.

[3] See *Le Temps*, 16 August 1928, for account of the proceedings at the Conference of Jurists, held at Salzburg in September 1928, to discuss the measures to be taken to unify the laws in both countries, regarding industrial and commercial cartels, etc.

[4] Article by Bauer, *Der Kampf*, July 1927: 'Es wird nicht das Reich Hindenburgs u. des Bürgerblocks sein, in das wir kommen werden.'

On the other hand, right-wing opinion in Austria was coming to view an *Anschluss* with less misgiving. Dr. Seipel, in particular, made speeches about this time which suggested that he had to some extent changed his views. These occasioned considerable misgiving in France, where he had always been regarded as the great supporter of Austrian independence. In September 1928 France issued a sharp warning: 'Un esprit aussi averti ne peut ignorer qu'en tout état de cause, le rattachement de l'Autriche à l'Allemagne, de quelque manière qu'on veuille poser le problème, ce serait la guerre pour toutes les puissances interessées au maintien du statu quo en Europe.' (*Le Temps*, 21 September 1928.)

really wanted. And opinion was finally disillusioned as to the efficacy of a democracy which was unable to give effect to what was felt to be the unmistakable wishes of the electorate, even when these were legally attainable, as most Austrians believed them to be. The fact that France and Czechoslovakia clearly meant to oppose the scheme, whether it was found to be legal or not; whether Austria and Germany desired it or not; and without any consideration for the possible economic advantages which might accrue to Austria, who was known to be in desperate need, was hardly calculated to strengthen the Austrians' not very fervent belief in the wisdom of constitutional government, of which Czechoslovakia and France were supposed to be among the chief exponents. After the failure of the Curtius-Schober project, subsequent efforts to bring about the *Anschluss* were diverted into extra-constitutional channels.

It had been hoped in certain Allied circles after the war that it might prove possible to find a solution to the Austrian problem in the formation of a democratic federation of Danubian states. Such an arrangement, it was felt, would not only help Austria but would provide an effective barricade against possible German aggression in south-eastern Europe in the future.[1] And the economic advantages of maintaining the old free-trade area of the Empire as far as possible intact were felt to be considerable.[2]

It was, however, never found possible to realize such a

[1] *War Memoirs of David Lloyd George*, Nicholson and Watson (London, 1936), vol. v, pp. 2463 *et seq.*:

'The downfall of Russia had created fresh anxiety for the political future of Europe, and it was feared in many influential quarters that unless some counterweight was established on the Continent to Germany in place of Russia, the future peace of Europe might continue to be precarious. . . . If Austria were prepared to play that role and break with Germany, she would have not only our sympathy, but our active support . . . our object now was to assist Austria to give the greatest freedom and autonomy to her subject nationalities." Mr. Lloyd George envisaged the development of a federation of free peoples in Central Europe, and hoped that in the future other peoples, not at that time a part of the Austro-Hungarian Empire, might be attracted into the orbit of the confederation.

[2] Article 222 of the Treaty of Versailles had provided for tariff agreements between Austria, Hungary, and Czechoslovakia. But when an attempt was made to realize these in 1921, it came to nothing, because of the opposition of Italy.

scheme. Germany, for obvious reasons, disliked it. Italy always opposed it, in whatever form it was proposed.[1] And the Austrians, though willing, and indeed anxious, to establish friendly relations with their neighbours, and to do as much trade as possible with them, could never consent to become an organic part of an organization of states potentially hostile to Germany. And apart from racial considerations, the intellectual and cultural life of Austria necessarily inclined her towards co-operation with the Western Powers.

The main obstacle to Danubian confederation, however, came from the states of the Little Entente themselves. For many months after the Armistice sporadic fighting had continued round the frontiers of Austria and Hungary, thus preventing any possibility of close co-operation. Even after this came to an end, it was inevitable that the Succession States would feel the need of time to consolidate their new territories, and that the last thing they would want, while doing this, would be to join forces again with their old rulers. It was this fear of an eventual resuscitation of Austria-Hungary which strengthened the bonds between Czechoslovakia, Roumania, and Yugoslavia. And the organization of the Little Entente, instead of becoming looser with the passage of time, as might have been expected, became progressively stronger. Even in 1932, for instance, when Austria and Hungary were both, economically, at their last gasp, this fear remained, and was instrumental in causing the failure of the Tardieu Plan.[2]

At the same time, it was realized, particularly in Czechoslovakia, that Austria must not be allowed to drift, in desperate defiance of the Treaties, into an *Anschluss* with Germany. Sufficient concessions must be made to make possible her continued existence as a weak but independent state.[3]

[1] Italy always viewed with misgiving any signs of an incipient *rapprochement* between Austria and the Little Entente, fearing the resuscitation of her old foe, the Empire, in new forms.

[2] See also speech of Beneš at the Bucharest Conference of the Little Entente, May 1925.

[3] Hence, the signing of the Treaty of Lana between Austria and Czechoslovakia in 1921. The economic position of Austria continued, however, to be unsatisfactory; and the Layton Rist report, published in 1926, stated that this condition of affairs was largely a consequence of the policy of economic nationalism pursued by the Succession States.

The Tardieu scheme was launched in order to try to escape from the obviously unsatisfactory and unstable existing state of affairs. The time appeared to be auspicious, for the *Anschluss* scheme had failed; and both Austria and her neighbours were in a very bad way economically.[1] Moreover, Austria had recently, of necessity, become peculiarly susceptible to French influence.[2] France had an obvious responsibility towards Austria, for she had taken the lead in opposition to the *Anschluss* scheme; and she had admitted, in her Constructive Memorandum of the spring of 1931 that the Powers must make themselves responsible for the future well-being of Austria.[3]

M. Tardieu's scheme[4] was not, however, well received by any of the interested parties.

In Austria, the fact that the scheme did not embrace Germany undoubtedly made it more palatable to many of the right-wing groups, who hoped that with a little luck Danubian Confederation might become synonymous with Habsburg

[1] The initiative came from the Austrian side. On 15 February 1932 Buresch solemnly declared to the assembled ambassadors of Great Britain, France, and Italy that Austria could not continue any longer under present conditions, as it was becoming increasingly difficult to trade with neighbouring states. Austria would, he said, be willing to enter into close economic negotiations with any and every state who would be willing to do so. (*Neue Freie Presse*, 16 February 1932.)

[2] Schober had been dropped in the January reshuffle of the Buresch cabinet; and the new Government was supported by all the groups who had come to regard the idea of an *Anschluss* with disfavour.

[3] 'The French Government considers that in view of the difficult position of Austria it is the duty of the Powers to which that country has given an undertaking not to alienate its independence, to contribute to its material development, on the understanding that Austria on her side will do all in her power to improve her economic situation.' (League of Nations VII, C. 338, M. 151, 1931 (C.E.U.E., 1933).)

[4] The scheme, as communicated in a Memorandum to the Governments of Great Britain and Italy on 2 March, took as its starting-point the official report of the 44th session of the Financial Committee of the League, which had drawn special attention to the critical position in Austria and Hungary. It comprised proposals that Austria, Hungary, and the Little Entente should arrange a preference scheme among themselves, and should form, as it were, a united bloc *vis-à-vis* the outside world. The great Powers were to allow the entry of Danubian agricultural products at preferential rates, without demanding any *quid pro quo*. (*L'Europe Nouvelle*, 2 April 1932, p. 445.)

Restoration.[1] The Social Democrats also, frustrated in their efforts to achieve the *Anschluss*, were comparatively well-disposed towards Tardieu's plan. There could, indeed, have been many worse solutions from the socialist point of view.[2]

At the same time, Austrian opinion as a whole cannot be described as enthusiastic, for it was all too obvious that the scheme had been conceived as an alternative to the *Anschluss*.

The economic advantages which would accrue to Austria were not too clear. It was feared, not without justification, that the struggling peasants of the Alpine Provinces would be unable to compete with the produce of the fertile Danubian states. And Austrian industrialists viewed with misgiving the prospect of Czech competition.

The attitude of the other proposed participants was not favourable. It was feared in the agricultural states (Hungary, Roumania, and Yugoslavia) that Austria and Czechoslovakia would not be able to absorb anything like all their surplus agricultural products.[3] And these three states maintained that in no circumstances could they give up extra-Danubian markets.

It is doubtful whether the scheme would have been of great value from the economic standpoint. The analogy of pre-war days was inapplicable, for, in the area which it was now

[1] The position of the *Heimwehr* and clerical groups was, however, difficult when it became apparent that the plan would not have the support of Italy, for these groups were probably, by this time, to a large extent dependent on Italian support.

[2] The *Prager Presse* of 23 September 1932, quoted at length from a recent article in *Der Kampf*, by Paul Szende, as follows: 'Es ist ein Irrtum, wenn man dieses Problem so darstellt, als ob Osterreich die Wahl zwischen Anschluss u. Donauföderation habe. Diese Wahl besteht zur Zeit überhaupt nicht. Es gibt vorlaüfig nur zwei Möglichkeiten: Donauföderation in einer Gestalt, bei welcher der französische Einfluss dominiert, oder Zusammenschluss einiger Staaten unter der militarischen Oberherrschaft des fascistischen Italien. Mit anderen Worten, die Wahl steht zwischen grosser oder kleiner Donauföderation frei.'

It was further pointed out that whereas the Small Plan would almost certainly lead to a return of the Habsburgs the Big Plan would not necessarily do so.

[3] Schober estimated that between one-sixth and one-seventh of the Danubian surplus might be absorbed, but that this would mean the ruin of Austrian and Czech agriculturists. (He was, however, including Bulgaria in this computation.) (*Frankfurter Zeitung*, 3 February 1932.)

proposed to amalgamate, agriculture formed a much larger proportion of the total economy than in the roughly corresponding pre-war area, in spite of the development of industry in the Succession States. Bessarabia and Serbia, wholly agricultural districts, were now included in the new area; and agriculture had been sedulously, and to a large extent successfully, fostered in Austrian and Czechoslovak districts where it had been of little or no importance before the war.

Moreover, the whole scheme looked rather like an attempt to set the clock back, for, from the League documents published about this time, on economic conditions in central Europe, it was clear that all the six Danubian states had, of recent years, had more trade with the western countries and less with each other.[1] And it was a dubious undertaking, from the economic point of view, to try to exclude Italy and Germany from Danubian markets, whatever might have been said for the attempt on political grounds.[2]

Thus the third possible 'democratic' solution for Austria proved to be unrealizable, on political, economic, and cultural grounds.

In fact the only foreign policy which appeared to be at all feasible by 1933 was one which was decidedly anti-democratic in its implications, namely an Italian policy.[3]

[1] In 1928, for instance, 35·5 per cent. of Danubian exports were within the Danubian group. By 1931, this proportion had dropped to 25·5 per cent.

[2] As regards Austria, for instance, while Hungary and the Little Entente took 29·5 per cent. of her exports, Germany and Italy took as much as 24·4 per cent. And as regards imports, the four Danubian states sent 36 per cent., while Germany and Italy sent 26·3 per cent. In each of the other Danubian states the position was essentially the same. (See *League Documents, Economic and Financial*, 1932, E. 781—'Études relatives au problème des rapprochements économiques. Chiffres essentiels du commerce exterieur des pays danubiens.') The group did not, indeed, form at all a satisfactory economic unit. Apart from the fact that Austria and Czechoslovakia could not absorb anything like all the surplus agricultural produce of the other three, their own industrial products tended to be of a kind that could only find a market in relatively highly developed countries. (This was especially the case with Austrian semi-luxury goods.)

[3] Italy's plans for Austria were, however, never very clearly defined, and probably varied considerably from time to time. Similarly, the groups susceptible to Italian influence, in Austria, all tended to have plans of their own.

From the first days of the Republic there had existed right-wing groups in Austria who were not reconciled to the new democratic régime,[1] and with these the Italian Government, dissatisfied with the attitude of the Allies, established connections, without, at first, any success.[2] In 1922, however, an opportunity arose, when Seipel, in desperation, visited the various capitals of Europe seeking for economic help, having warned the Powers, at the London Conference, that unless they were prepared to come to Austria's assistance, they must take over her administration themselves. When he met the Italian Foreign Minister, Schantzer, at Verona, on 24 October 1922, it was proposed that a customs union should be formed between the two countries; and that Italy should take over the control of Austrian finances. The union was evidently intended to be relatively far-reaching. It is not, however, clear from which side the initiative came. Schantzer in any case hesitated, and the League stepped into the breach.[3]

During the next few years, the possibility of any kind of Italian solution receded as the relationship between the two

[1] These groups were recruited, in the main, from the ranks of the old Imperial Army, the Church, and the aristocracy.

[2] In the years immediately following the Armistice, for instance, she probably lent her support to the somewhat nebulous schemes then afoot for the formation of a south-German Catholic state under one of the Wittelsbachs. This state was to include Bavaria, Austria, Hungary, and possibly Croatia. The plan was apparently sponsored by Austrian clerical circles, certain French circles, and by the Vatican. The scheme, however, came to nothing. (C. A. Macartney, 'The Armed Formations of Austria', *Journal of the Institute of International Affairs*, vol. viii (1929), pp. 167 *et seq.*)

[3] The question arose again, at the time when the Austro-German Customs Union proposal was being considered by the International Court. Herr Kaufmann, the Austrian representative, then distinguished between 'associations douanières' and 'inclusions douanières'. The proposal of 1922 was, he said, an example of the latter: 'Il n'y a pas de doute quant du point de savoir que ce projet aurait compromis l'independence de l'Autriche au sens de l'article 88 de S. Germain.' The initiative had, he indicated, come from Italy. The Italian representative, M. Pilotti, denied this, however: 'Le gouvernement autrichien . . . a envoyé ses représentants en Italie pour proposer au gouvernement italien de prendre à sa charge la monnaie autrichienne, et de faire une Union douanière aussi complète que possible. Cette proposition n'a pas été acceptée par le gouvernement italien; on a estimé que la charge aurait été lourde pour les finances italiennes de cette époque.' (*Cour Permanente de Justice Internationale Série C*, No. 53, pp. 525 *et seq.* Also Muriel Curry, *Italian Foreign Policy* (Nicholson and Watson, 1932), p. 73.)

countries degenerated into one of positive hostility over the question of the South Tyrol.[1] And it was long remembered against Italy that she had supported Hungary's claim to a plebiscite in Odenburg in 1921.

But although the greater part of the population continued, as in pre-war days, to dislike and despise the Italians, Italy found plenty of opportunity for mischief-making. The *Heimwehr*, for instance, originally founded to keep the peace and defend the frontiers in Carinthia and Styria, shared from the beginning the Italian dislike of Yugoslavia. And with the advent of Mussolini in Italy, and the growth of reactionary forces within the *Heimwehr*, the link with Italy became stronger. As early as 1927, for instance, it was rumoured that the more extreme of the parties of the right, whose dislike of the Social Democrats predominated over their concern at the plight of the South Tyrol, were willing to play Italy's game in return for material support for the *Heimwehr*.[2]

If it is uncertain to what extent Seipel's Government felt positive sympathy for Italy, it is certainly true that Austria was not in a position to ignore her, for, in conjunction with her enthusiastic ally, Hungary, she was in a position to exert a very formidable pressure on Austria. This was shown very clearly at the time of the riots of July 1927. Italian support of Hungarian revisionist aspirations, which were at that time concentrated on the *Burgenland*, was well known. And Hun-

[1] The German minority in the South Tyrol had, since 1923, been subjected to systematic Italianization. This had been the subject of much indignant comment in Germany and Austria. Vigorous protest from the Bavarian Premier, Dr. Held, in 1926, elicited an extremely belligerent speech from Mussolini, in which he remarked that in no circumstances would Italy withdraw her flag from the Brenner. She might even, if need be, carry it further.

[2] *Manchester Guardian*, 5 November 1927, quoting from *Vorwärts*, the *Deutschen Volkswirt*, and the *Münchener Neueste Nachrichten*.

On 5 November the *Frankfurter Zeitung* drew attention in a long article to widespread rumours to the effect that the *Heimwehr* was being financed with Italian gold, and provided with Italian weapons. The Styrian *Landeshauptmann*, Rintelen, it was pointed out, had entertained the closest political and financial relations with Italy since he had given over the Styrian Water Power Company to Italian capital. Italy, it was suggested, would like to be able to control Styria because it would enable her more effectively to encircle Yugoslavia.

gary would have required little encouragement to step in and take what she claimed was her own.[1] This state of affairs persisted through 1928. Relations with Italy continued, in spite of the danger, or perhaps because of it, to be uncertain.[2] But, as the right became progressively stronger in Austria, the anti-Italian tide began to turn.[3]

It was not, however, until 1930 that Schober finally established the relationship of the two countries on a positively friendly basis, by his visit to Rome in the February of that year.[4] The *rapprochement* was inevitably something of a Canossa for Austria,[5] and it speaks well for Schober's statesmanship that the visit did not arouse a great deal more opposition in Austria than was actually the case. It is probable that Schober himself did not intend the Italian visit to inaugurate the beginning of a new trend in Austrian foreign policy.[6] The French, however, and the Italians themselves, did not hesitate to assert that it did.[7]

The influence of Italy in Austrian politics had certainly

[1] Hungary's relations with her other neighbours had been rather more friendly in 1925 and 1926. The possibilities of opposition to a forward policy in the *Burgenland* had therefore decreased.

[2] The position of the South Tyrol, for instance, was discussed with great bitterness in the National Council in February.

[3] At the beginning of July 1928, for instance, Seipel made overtures to Italy by admitting that the point at issue in the Alto Adige was simply a cultural one. The Italian minister, absent since February, returned forthwith to Vienna.

[4] Schober went primarily in order to thank Italy for her recent support at the Hague, but also to conclude a Treaty of Friendship and Arbitration.

[5] Schober had, for instance, to walk in the funeral procession of one M. Bianchi, a well-known Austrian irredentist of pre-war days. (*Kölnische Zeitung*, 11 February 1930.)

[6] In his speech in the National Council, Schober remarked that 'der Vertrag mit dem Königreich Italien ist in seiner Tendenz die gradlinige Fortführung der Politik Österreichs, mit allen Staaten in friedliche Beziehungen zu leben.' (*Reichspost*, 26 February 1930.)

[7] '. . . L'Autriche est considerée comme un anneau' (between Italy and Hungary) 'qui pourrait rendre du précieux services au nouveau système italien d'alliances et d'amities.' (*Le Temps*, 8 February 1930.) 'Le gouvernement fasciste paraît, en tout cas, faire un nouvel effort pour organiser sur le Danube un groupe capable de contre-balancer l'influence de la Petite-Éntente, et de créer au centre de l'Europe, une situation politique correspondant aux idées et à l'intérêt italiens.' (*Le Temps*, 8 February 1930: also *Pester Lloyd*, 26 February 1930.)

increased considerably by 1930. This was in part a consequence of the fact that, for reasons of internal politics, the balance of power in Austria had passed to the right-wing groups, who had natural affinities with both the civil and the ecclesiastical powers in Italy. There can be little doubt that the fact that Italy was ready to back these materially as well as morally gave them eventually an advantage over the left and the centre which they might never otherwise have acquired.[1]

The pattern of Austrian foreign policy, long veiled in obscurity, was now becoming clear. The 1931 Customs Union proposals had showed that the great body of democratic and moderate feeling in the country still looked for salvation in union with the Reich. The Social Democrats were certainly becoming more doubtful of the advisability of an *Anschluss* in the immediate future, in view of events in Germany. But their lack of enthusiasm was made up for by the fervour of the Nazi group, which was growing rapidly.[2]

The right-wing clerical group, whose interests were more or less identical with those of a large section of the *Heimwehr*,[3] would probably have had little chance of maturing their plans, even after the failure of the 1931 Customs Union project, had it not been for the support which they received from Italy and

[1] The author of *Alarmruf aus Österreich*, a well-informed pamphlet which appeared in 1931, and emanated, apparently, from someone in close proximity to Schober, considered that Austrian reactionary groups would probably be of negligible importance were they not supported from outside the country.

[2] It would be easy to expatiate at length on the unsuitability of the Nazi ideology for Austria. But the movement had, none the less, much to recommend it in Austrian eyes. It was anti-democratic, at a time when disillusionment with democracy was widespread; it was anti-clerical, a factor of great importance in Austria where anti-clericalism is much more widely spread than is commonly supposed; and it was pro-German. It was thus, superficially at any rate, admirably suited in many respects as a creed for the impoverished, free-thinking middle class. And it recruited its hangers-on for the purposes of demonstrations, fights, etc., from the army of the down-and-outs, who were ready to work and fight for anyone who paid them, and to believe in any party which worked against the existing régime, and held out sufficiently alluring promises of future wealth.

[3] A considerable part of the *Heimwehr*, notably in Styria, were Nazi in sympathy.

the Vatican. The aristocracy and the army, from whom these groups were mainly recruited, had never had deep roots in Austria; they had lived, both before and after the war, in a closed circle, as a class apart from the people. On the other hand, the return of the Habsburgs to Austria and Hungary, which was the more or less constant aim of these groups, was a policy eminently acceptable to Italy (though the Right-wing parties no doubt anticipated being in a position to dispense with Italian 'advice', once they were established). And Great Britain, irritated by the insistent demands of nervous French imperialists, would probably have been glad enough if Italy could have taken the place of France in building up a strong bloc in south-eastern Europe, which would in its nature constitute a permanent check on German ambitions. Even France, too much embroiled in her own difficulties to be able to finance much longer the costly experiment of Austrian 'independence', was able to view Italian schemes without undue alarm. And some circles in Czechoslovakia, the senior partner in the Little Entente, were coming to believe that Italian influence, even if this meant a return of the Habsburgs, was a lesser evil than the *Anschluss*.

Italian schemes at first took the form of the encouragement of a *rapprochement* between Austria and Hungary. In July 1930 Schober made a journey to Budapest. The two countries exchanged mutual compliments; and the tension that had existed between them before and after the war was conveniently forgotten.[1] Too much significance should not, however, be attached to this visit.

There appears, however, to be reason for believing that the relationship between the two countries became very much closer during the short period of office of the Seipel–Vaugoin minority Government in the autumn, and it was widely be-

[1] Report of Count Bethlen's speech, at a dinner given in Schober's honour when he visited Budapest: 'Viele Jahrhunderte gemeinsamer Friedensarbeit . . . unzählige gemeinsame Kämpfe, gemeinsam vergossenes Blut, ebenso wie die letzten zehn Jahre gemeinsam erduldeten Leiden . . . sind ein festes Band, das uns mit unserem österreichischen Nachbar in warmer Freundschaft verbindet.' (*Neues Wiener Tageblatt*, 8 July 1930.)

lieved that the question of a military alliance at least was then discussed, although this was officially denied.[1]

In March and April interest in the Hungarian question was overshadowed by the German Customs Union proposals. It was revived, however, at the beginning of May, by an unofficially inspired article which appeared in the *Tribuna*, in which Italy gave it to be understood that she considered that Austria's true mission was to remain as a Danubian state, closely linked with Hungary.[2]

The Hungarian project probably came to be viewed with increasing favour in the course of the summer in certain Austrian circles,[3] as it was becoming ever more apparent that the Customs Union would not be realized. And French and

[1] The *Frankfurter Zeitung* of 1 February 1931 quoted an article from the *Österreichische Volkswirt* as follows: 'Vor dem Wechsel auf dem Ballhausplatz, hätte Bethlen mit gutem Grunde auf einen Wortlaut rechnen können, der über den üblichen Freundschaftsvertrag hinausgegangen wäre. Auch das wäre natürlich ein rein defensiver Vertrag gewesen, aber doch immerhin, ein Vertrag auf mehr als bloss formalen Inhalt.' The *Frankfurter Zeitung* commented on this as follows: 'Dass die Politik Seipels in dieser Richtung gelassen ist, u. dass die reaktionären Kreise . . . nichts lieber sehen würden als einen Anschluss Österreichs an das halbdiktatorisch regierte Ungarn u. seine Gruppe, besteht kein Zweifel.'

[2] The article was quoted in *Le Temps* of 4 May 1931 as follows: 'La mission historique, économique et politique de l'Autriche est du reste en fonction danubienne. C'est pourquoi c'est seulement avec une autre pays typiquement danubienne, la Hongrie, que l'Autriche peut améliorer sa structure économique, renforcer son entité politique, et acquérir de l'autorité en Europe . . . l'Italie trouverait dans ce nouvel équilibre de l'Europe centrale et balkanique un précieux facteur, pour le développement de sa politique de paix et d'expansion, et la France un moyen efficace pour éviter l'Anschluss.'

[3] The *Weltblatt*, for instance, representing the views of Herr Kunschak and the more liberal wing of the Christian Socialist party, remarked that 'la necessité s'impose à l'Autriche de se préparer, ou tout au moins de ne pas s'opposer, à son union qui est trés prochain, avec la Hongrie. Lorsque l'évolution, qui est imminente, arrivera à son terme, les deux peuples seront peut-être accessibles à l'idée d'un restauration de la Monarchie.' (Quoted in *Le Temps*, 26 October 1931.)

On 22 November 1931 the project was discussed at a meeting of the *Wiener Industriellenklub*, at which leading business men from both countries were present. (*Pester Lloyd*, 22 November 1931.)

The matter was broached in Parliament about this time, in connection with the negotiations which had taken place between Dr. Dollfuss, Minister of Agriculture, and M. Hantos, the Hungarian Minister of Trade. The project was opposed by the National Economic Bloc. (*Neue Freie Presse*, 24 November 1931.)

Czech opinion was coming to feel that even the Habsburg solution would be preferable to that of an *Anschluss* between Austria and Germany.[1]

Italy, however, always uncertain as to her best line of attack, showed some hesitation when the question of Danubian Federation came up in 1932. It was not until the time of the London Conference that she decided definitely to oppose this plan.

The moment appeared an opportune one for the Italian scheme, for those of the *Heimwehr* who had not openly or secretly gone over to the Nazis now appeared to rally round the Legitimist cause.[2] Italy now openly supported the *Heimwehr*.[3] The Church also came out openly in favour of it, and it became quite usual for *Heimwehr* meetings to begin with an open-air Mass.[4]

Negotiations with Hungary were not, however, found to be very easy. And even the attempt to negotiate a new commercial treaty in the summer of 1932 occasioned much difficulty and ill-feeling.

At the end of 1932 the old project of the formation of a

[1] Article in *Frankfurter Zeitung*, 29 August 1931: 'Man glaubt, dass den Franzosen, aber auch den Italienern, ein Zusammenschluss mit Ungarn unter einem Habsburger als ein kleineres Übel als der Anschluss Österreichs an Deutschland erscheinen werde. Auch die Kleine Entente ist in der ablehnenden Haltung gegenüber Habsburg . . . nicht mehr so einig wie früher.'

[2] Article by Léon Blum in *Populaire*, 3 November 1932: 'La Heimwehr d'Autriche, en partie Hitlerienne, reste en grande majorité hapsbourgeoise. Elle entretient les plus étroites relations avec le gouvernement fasciste de Hongrie, avec les Casques d'Acier, avec Mussolini. Le Ministre d'Italie n'a pas craint de figurer publiquement à la dernière manifestation des Heimwehren.' Léon Blum pointed out that these people were gradually getting into government circles, and that Major Fey, for instance, belonged to them.

[3] On 15 and 16 October, for instance, when a conference of *Heimwehr* leaders was held in Vienna, at which 1,000 *Heimwehr* men appeared, the Italian minister was present. (*Le Temps*, 17 October 1932.)

[4] *Alarmruf aus Österreich*, 1931: 'Dass Fascismus u. Vatikan in Ungarn u. Österreich gemeinsam marschieren, ist allein aus dem Wohlwollen der österreichischen Kirchenfürsten für die von Mussolini begönnerten Heimwehren erwiesen. Der österreichische u. ungarische Legitimismus wird nahezu von allen Kardinälen, Bischöfen, Prälaten u. Aebten dieser beider Länder ganz offen begünstigt. Das wäre ohne Zustimmung des Oberherrn in Rom nicht möglich.'

South German Catholic state which was to include Austria, Hungary, and Bavaria was revived unofficially. It is, however, doubtful if the scheme ever approached actuality, although Dr. Dollfuss was said to be interested in it.[1]

In conclusion, it may be said that in the early post-war years, when both Austria's friends and her principal creditors were democratic states, the signs of reaction in Austria were relatively few. But the movement of Germany towards the right, round about 1928, inevitably led to a similar movement in Austria; and at the same time France, and, to a lesser extent, the satellite Little Entente states, timorous before the increasing power of Germany, came to view with ever less aversion a solution of the Austrian problem on the lines envisaged by the right-wing Austrian groups. A development of this kind was by no means wholly to their liking, but it at least precluded, so they thought, the menace of the *Anschluss*.

Thus Austria's democratic friends came to view with comparative equanimity the increasingly large part played by Italy in Austrian affairs from 1930 onwards. Italy, it was thought, could be trusted to play for all time an anti-German game. This she undoubtedly did, as long as she was able. But the price which had to be paid was the sacrifice of democratic government.[2]

It was, from the first, all too obvious that Austria was considered by the great Powers as a pawn in the game of international politics, and that the right of self-determination would never be accorded her. It was, therefore, not unnatural that, as the years went on, the country ceased to desire the maintenance of a sham 'independence'.

[1] Meetings were held on 11 November and 12 November 1932 in Salzburg, at which both Dr. Dollfuss and Dr. Held, the Bavarian Premier, were present. And the *Heimwehr* and the Bavarian Casques d'Acier held joint manœuvres at Salzach, at the beginning of December.

[2] The crushing of the Social Democrats, in February 1934, for instance, was probably a direct result of Italian intervention.

CONCLUSION

IN conclusion, an attempt may be made to sum up very briefly some of the main causes for the breakdown of democratic government in Austria.

The constitution of 1920 undoubtedly played its part, for the omnipotence of parliament which it set out to effect became in fact the omnipotence of the party organizations. Every issue was treated as a party issue, and every aspect of life came to be tinged with political disputes. Parliament, which should have operated to draw the rival groups together, accentuated the differences between them.

It is not suggested that all or even most of the disasters which befell the Austrian Republic can be attributed to defects of the constitution. Constitutions can help or hinder the success of democracy; they do not generally in themselves decide the fate of democratic government. In Austria the unwise provisions of the 1920 constitution probably only served to accentuate difficulties which might well have proved to be insuperable in any case.

The unsatisfactory economic condition of the country, for instance, fostered, as it always must, the growth of extremism on both sides.[1] It prevented the people from developing any feeling of pride in the new Austria, which came to be associated for them with economic misery such as they had never known before.

Again, their experiences in the sphere of foreign policy did nothing to generate an Austrian patriotism in the people. These rather served to indicate to them their helplessness in the face of a hostile world, and the futility of maintaining the façade of self-government when in fact the country was tied hand and foot by its creditors. Self-government was but another name for the administration of the country by the Allies.

Finally, it may be said that so long as democratic govern-

[1] The more perspicacious of the Social Democrats understood the danger well. (See speech of Seitz at the 1930 Party Conference.)

ment lasted in Germany, Austrian democrats had little to fear. But the combination of the collapse of parliamentary democracy in the Reich with the necessity of turning to Fascist Italy for support against the Nazi terror, led inevitably to the collapse of parliamentary democracy in Austria.

APPENDIX A

The Evolution of the Constitution

March 1919–October 1920

March 1919

Renner entrusted Professor Kelsen, the Constitutional Adviser to the Legislative Department of the Chancery, with the task of drawing up a new constitution.

May 1919

Dr. Mayr, on behalf of the Christian Socialists, produced a draft constitution.

October 1919

Dr. Mayr worked, on behalf of the Christian Socialist–Social Democrat coalition government, at projects for constitutional and administrative reform. Finally, he drew up a draft constitution, which he used as a basis in his negotiations with the political parties in the Provinces.

January 1920

A Provincial Conference was held at Salzburg to consider the question of the new constitution. No government officials, except Dr. Mayr, were invited to be present. Dr. Mayr presented his project as a personal one, and it was adopted as a basis for discussion. It represented, on the whole, a compromise between Christian Socialist and Social Democratic views, although its bias not unnaturally tended towards the former.

February 1920

A second Provincial Conference was held at Linz. Dr. Mayr's project, which had in the meantime been remodelled to some extent in favour of the Social Democrats, was again adopted as the basis for discussion and some progress was made. The Social Democrats, however, repeatedly emphasized the fact that these conferences could not be regarded as official, and that the only body by which definitive decisions could be reached was the National Assembly.

May 1920

Dr. Dinghofer produced a draft constitution on behalf of the German Nationalists.[1]

7 July 1920

Dr. Mayr produced a second draft constitution.[2]

Herr Abraham produced the first Social Democrat draft constitution.[3]

15 July 1920

The Constitutional Committee of the 'Proporz' Cabinet appointed a sub-committee of seven members with Dr. Kelsen as Constitutional Adviser.

24 September 1920

This body, after much discussion and consultation with other bodies, presented their project to the Constitutional Committee on 24 September.[4]

1 October 1920

This draft constitution was laid before the Constituent Assembly just before its term of office expired, in October 1920.

[1] Beilage, Nr. 842. [2] Beilage, Nr. 888. [3] Beilage, Nr. 904.

[4] See 'Bericht des Verfassungsausschusses über den Entwurf eines Gesetzes, womit die Republik Österreich als Bundesstaat eingerichtet wird. Beilagen zum stenographischen Protokoll der Konstituirender Nationalversammlung'. (Kelsen, *Verfassungsgesetze*, Bd. V, pp. 501 *et seq.*)

APPENDIX B

Law of 1 October 1920
constituting
THE REPUBLIC OF AUSTRIA
as a
FEDERAL STATE
(Federal Constitutional Law)

The National Assembly has resolved:

FIRST SECTION

GENERAL PROVISIONS

Article 1

Austria is a democratic Republic. Its law emanates from the people.

Article 2

(1) Austria is a Federal State.

(2) The Federal State shall consist of the following Provinces: Burgenland, Carinthia, Lower Austria (Province of Lower Austria and Vienna), Upper Austria, Salzburg, Styria, Tyrol, and Vorarlberg.

Article 3

(1) The Federal territory embraces the territories of the Federal Provinces.

(2) An alteration in the Federal territory involving an alteration in the territory of a Province or an alteration in a Provincial frontier within the Federal territory (otherwise than by peace treaties) can be made only by identical Constitutional Laws of the Federation and of the Province the territory of which is altered.

(3) Special provisions applicable to the Province of Lower Austria and Vienna are contained in the Fourth Section.

Article 4

(1) The Federal territory constitutes a uniform territory for purposes of defence, economic affairs, and customs.

(2) Internal customs barriers or other restrictions to intercourse shall not be set up within the Federation.

Article 5

The Federal capital and seat of the supreme Federal Government offices is Vienna.

Article 6

(1) There shall be a provincial citizenship for each Province. The qualification requisite for provincial citizenship shall be the right of domicile in a commune of the Province. The conditions under which provincial citizenship shall be acquired and lost shall be the same in every Province.

(2) Federal citizenship shall be acquired by the act of acquiring provincial citizenship.

(3) Every citizen of the Federation shall have in each Province the same rights and duties as the citizens of the Province.

Article 7

(1) All citizens of the Federation shall be equal before the law. Privileges of birth, sex, position, class, and religion are abolished.

(2) Public officials, including members of the Federal Army, shall enjoy the unimpaired exercise of their political rights.

Article 8

The German language shall be the official language of the Republic, but without prejudice to the rights accorded by Federal laws to linguistic minorities.

Article 9

The universally recognized rules of international law shall be constituent parts of the Law of the Federation.

Article 10

Legislative and executive power in regard to the following matters is vested in the Federation:

(1) The Federal Constitution, especially elections to the National Council, plebiscites based upon the Federal Constitution; constitutional jurisdiction;

(2) Foreign affairs, including political and economic representation abroad, and especially the conclusion of all political treaties; the limitation of boundaries; foreign trade in goods and live stock; customs;

(3) Regulation and supervision of entrance into the Federal territory and departure thence; immigration and emigration; passport system; removal, dismissal, banishment, and extradition from the Federal territory, and the granting of permission to pass through the Federal territory;

(4) Federal finances, especially public taxes, exclusively or partially collected for the Federation; monopolies;

(5) Currency, credit, exchange, and banking; weights, measures, standards, and gauges;

(6) Civil law, including company law; criminal law, exclusive of the administrative penal law and administrative penal procedure in matters falling within the sphere of independent activity of the Provinces; the administration of justice; administrative jurisdiction; copyright; public press; expropriation, in so far as it does not concern matters falling within the sphere of independent activity of the Provinces; matters concerning solicitors, barristers, and allied professions;

(7) The law of associations and of assemblies;

(8) Matters concerning trade and industry; combating unfair competition; patents and the protection of patterns, marks, and other distinguishing signs on goods; matters concerning patent agents; engineering and civil technology; chambers of commerce, trade, and industry;

(9) Transport as regards railways, shipping, and air transit; matters connected with street railways, which, on account of their importance in connection with transit traffic, have

been declared by Federal law to be Federal routes; river and shipping police; posts, telegraphs, and telephones;

(10) Mining; control and maintenance of waterways navigable by boats or timber-rafts, and of waterways forming the boundary with a foreign country or between Provinces, or which flow between two or more Provinces; construction and maintenance of waterways connecting home with foreign territory or a number of Provinces with one another; general technical measures for the proper utilization of water power, excluding agricultural and small industrial works; fixation of standards and types of electrical plant and apparatus, and safety measures in connection therewith; high power supply legislation where the distributing installation extends to two or more Provinces; steam boilers and power machinery; surveying;

(11) Labour laws and protection of workpeople and employees, with the exception of agricultural and forestry workers and officials; social insurance and contract insurance;

(12) Public hygiene, excluding interments, the disposal of corpses, and sanitary services and life-saving services maintained by Communes; hospitals, convalescent homes, health resorts, and medicinal springs in respect of hygienic supervision only; veterinary services; food supply, including food control;

(13) Scientific and expert services in public archives and libraries; matters concerned with artistic and scientific collections and equipment; protection of monuments; religious matters; census of population and other statistics, in so far as they do not serve only the interests of a single Province; foundations and endowments, where such foundations and endowments are devoted to purposes which are not the exclusive concern of a single Province and have not hitherto been administered autonomously by the Provinces;

(14) Federal police and Federal gendarmerie;

(15) Military matters; losses due to war, care of persons who have served in war and of their dependants; measures

deemed necessary (owing to war or the results of war) for ensuring uniform control over economic affairs, particularly in regard to the provision of the necessaries of life for the people;

(16) Organization of Federal administrative and other authorities; service law for Federal officials.

Article 11

(1) Legislative power shall be vested in the Federation and executive power in the Provinces, in regard to the following matters:

a. Citizenship and right of domicile; matters of personal status, including registration and change of name; foreign police;
b. Occupational representation in so far as not included in Article 10, excluding agricultural and forestry representation;
c. Public agencies and private commercial agencies;
d. As regards public taxation not exclusively or partially levied for the Federation: measures to prevent double taxation or other excessive burdens, to prevent impediments to commercial intercourse or economic relations with foreign countries or between the Provinces or parts of Provinces, to prevent the imposition of charges, which are excessive or likely to impede traffic, upon the use of public traffic routes and appliances, and to prevent injury to the finances of the Federation;
e. Munitions, firearms, and explosives, in so far as these are not a monopoly, and weapons; automobiles;
f. Housing of the people.
g. Administration and administrative penal law, including compulsory execution and general determination of the administrative penal law, including matters in which Provincial legislation is applicable.

(2) Regulations giving effect to laws promulgated under the terms of paragraph (1) shall be issued by the Federation, unless otherwise provided by the laws themselves.

Article 12

(1) Legislative power in respect of principles shall be vested in the Federation and the enactment of executive decrees and executive power shall be vested in the Provinces in regard to the following matters:

a. Organization of the administration of the Provinces;
b. Poor relief; population policy; popular sanatoria; care of mothers, infants, and children; hospital and nursing-homes, health resorts, and medicinal springs;
c. Institutions for the protection of society against criminal, neglected, or otherwise dangerous persons, such as compulsory labour and similar institutions; removal and expulsion from one Province to another;
d. Public institutions for the settlement of disputes otherwise than by the Courts;
e. Labour laws and protection of workpeople and employees where such workpeople and employees are engaged in agriculture and forestry;
f. Land reform, especially agrarian operations and re-colonization;
g. Forestry, including pasturage; protection of plants against diseases and pests;
h. Electrical power supply and water rights, in so far as these are not included in Article 10;
i. Building;
j. Service regulations for Provincial officials exercising administrative authority.

(2) The decision, by way of final appeal, in matters connected with land reform (Par. 1 f) shall be entrusted to a Commission appointed by the Federation, and composed of Judges, administrative officers, and experts.

Article 13

(1) Legislative and executive power shall be vested in the Federation in regard to the allocation of taxes between the Federation, the Provinces, and the Communes, the apportionment of the share of the Provinces and of the Communes in the Federal receipts, and the determination of the contributions

and payments to be made from Federal funds towards the expenditure of the Provinces and Communes.

(2) Legislative and executive power shall be be vested in the Provinces in regard to the allocation of Provincial taxes to the Communes, the apportionment of the share of the Communes in the Provincial receipts, and the determination of the contributions and payments from Provincial funds towards the expenditure of the Communes.

Article 14

The spheres of action of the Federation and the Provinces in the domain of education, instruction, and national culture shall be determined by a special Federal Constitutional law.

Article 15

(1) In so far as legislative and executive power in respect of any matter is not expressly vested in the Federation, it shall remain within the sphere of independent action of the Provinces.

(2) In so far as legislation upon principles only is reserved to the Federation, the detailed execution shall be determined by legislation by the Provinces within the limits laid down by the Federal laws. The Federal law may fix a period for the promulgation of such implementary laws, the period to be not less than six months and not more than one year, save with the sanction of the Federal Council. Should this period be exceeded by any Province, the Federation shall become competent to promulgate the implementary laws for that Province. As soon as the Province has issued the implementary law, the implementary law of the Federation shall cease to be of effect.

(3) If an executive act by a Province in connection with the matters dealt with in Articles 11 and 12 is to become effective in several Provinces, the Provinces concerned must, in the first place, take steps to come to an agreement. Should they be unable to agree on the proposal of one of the Provinces, the appropriate Federal Ministry shall become competent to perform the act. Further provisions as to such cases may be

made by Federal laws issued in accordance with Articles 11 and 12.

(4) In matters reserved for Federal legislation in accordance with Articles 11 and 12, the Federation shall be entitled to enforce the observance of instructions issued by it.

(5) The Provinces shall be entitled, within the sphere of their legislative powers, to determine matters necessary to the carrying out of their objects, including matters of penal and civil law.

Article 16

(1) The Provinces shall be bound to take any measures which may be necessary, within their independent sphere of action, to give effect to political treaties; should a Province fail to fulfil this obligation punctually, the power to take such measures, and especially to enact the necessary laws, shall be transferred to the Federation.

(2) Similarly the Federation shall be entitled to supervise the carrying into effect of treaties with foreign States, even in matters falling within the sphere of independent action of the Provinces. In this connection the Federation shall enjoy the same rights with respect to the Provinces as in matters of indirect Federal administration (Article 102).

Article 17

(1) The position of the Federation as the holder of private rights under the Civil Law shall not be in any way affected by the provisions of Articles 10 to 15 as to competence in legislation and execution.

(2) The Federation may never, in all these legal relations, be placed by the legislation of any Province in a less favourable position than the Province itself.

Article 18

(1) The entire State administration may be carried on only upon the basis of the laws.

(2) Each administrative authority may issue orders within its own sphere of action, and in accordance with the laws.

Article 19

(1) The executive administration of the Federation and of the Provinces shall be entrusted to People's Commissioners appointed by the people's representatives in the Federation and in the Provinces. The People's Commissioners shall consist of the President of the Federation, the Federal Ministers, the Secretaries of State, and the members of the Provincial Governments.

(2) The proceedings of the People's Commissioners shall be under the supervision of the people's representatives by whom they were appointed.

(3) They may be summoned before the Constitutional Court to answer for their actions and omissions, in accordance with the terms of the Federal or Provincial Constitutions.

Article 20

The Federal or Provincial administration shall be carried on, in accordance with the law, by the various administrative departments, permanent or temporary, under the direction of the People's Commissioners. Unless otherwise provided by the Constitution of the Federation or the Provinces, these administrative departments shall be bound to obey the instructions of the People's Commissioners to whom they are subordinate, who shall be responsible for the carrying out of their official duties.

Article 21

(1) The conditions of service, including the salary system and disciplinary rules, of the officials of the Federation and of the Provinces who have administrative duties to perform (Article 10, paragraph 16, and Article 12, paragraph 10) shall be regulated upon uniform principles by Federal law. In particular, the law shall determine the extent to which staff representatives shall participate, without prejudice to the authority of the Federation and the Provinces, in the regulation of the rights and duties of these officials.

(2) The authority of the Federation in regard to its officials shall be exercised by the Federal People's Commissioners, that

of the Provinces in regard to their officials shall be exercised by the Provincial People's Commissioners.

(3) The appointment and conditions of service of officials of District and Local Communes performing administrative duties shall be regulated in conformity with the organization of the administrative services.

(4) The possibility of interchange of service between the Federation, the Provinces, and the Communes shall at all times be open to public officials. The transfer shall be effected by agreement with the departments appointed to exercise authority in staff matters. Federal legislation to prescribe special arrangements to facilitate interchange of service can be made.

(5) Official titles for the public services of the Federation, the Provinces, and the Communes may be determined by Federal law in a uniform manner. They shall be protected by law.

Article 22

All public services of the Federation, the Provinces, and the Communes shall be bound to give mutual assistance to one another within the limits of their several legitimate fields of action.

Article 23

(1) All persons entrusted with administrative duties under the Federation, the Provinces, or the Communes, or with judicial duties shall be liable for every breach of the law committed in the course of their duties, whether intentionally or by negligence, to the injury of any person whatsoever. The Federation, the Provinces, or the Communes shall be responsible for breaches of the law committed by the officials appointed by them.

(2) Further provisions in this respect shall be made by Federal law.

SECOND SECTION

FEDERAL LEGISLATION

I. The National Council

Article 24

Federal laws shall be passed by the National Council, elected by the people of the entire Federation, acting in conjunction with the Federal Council, elected by the Provincial Diets.

Article 25

(1) The seat of the National Council shall be the Federal Capital, Vienna.

(2) During the continuance of extraordinary circumstances, the President of the Federation may, at the request of the Federal Government, summon the National Council to meet in another place.

Article 26

(1) The National Council shall be elected by the people of the Federation on the basis of the equal, direct, secret, and personal suffrage of men and women who, before 1 January of the year in which the election takes place, have passed their twentieth year, and in accordance with the principles of proportional representation.

(2) The Federal territory shall be divided into self-contained electoral districts within the boundaries of the Provinces. The number of representatives to be elected by the electors in each electoral district (the electoral body) shall be proportionate to the number of citizens in that electoral district, that is, to the number of citizens of the Federation who according to the latest census of the population were ordinarily domiciled in the electoral district. Any division of the electorate into other electoral bodies is prohibited.

(3) The election day must be a Sunday or other public holiday.

(4) Any elector who has attained his twenty-fourth year

before 1 January of the year of the election shall be eligible for election.

(5) Deprivation of the right to vote and to be eligible for election may take place only as the result of a judicial sentence or decree.

Article 27

(1) The legislative period of the National Council shall last for four years, reckoned from the day of its first meeting, and in any case until the day on which the new National Council meets.

(2) The newly elected Council shall be summoned by the President of the Federation within not more than 30 days after the date of the election, which shall be so arranged by the Federal Government that the newly elected National Council may meet on the day after the expiration of the fourth year of the legislative period.

Article 28

The National Council may be adjourned only by its own decision. The summons to reassemble shall be issued by its Chairman. The Chairman shall be bound to summon the National Council immediately if so requested by at least one-fourth of its members or by the Federal Government.

Article 29

Before the expiration of the legislative period, the National Council may dissolve itself by merely passing a law to that effect. Even in such a case, the legislative period shall last until the assembling of the newly elected National Council.

Article 30

(1) The National Council shall elect from among its own numbers the Chairman, Vice-Chairman, and Deputy Vice-Chairman.

(2) The business of the National Council shall be conducted on the basis of a special law and in accordance with rules of procedure to be drawn up by the National Council itself in

accordance with that law. For the adoption of the law as to the conduct of business the presence of half the members and a majority of two-thirds of the votes cast are necessary.

Article 31

For a valid decision to be taken by the National Council the presence of at least one-third of the members and an absolute majority of the votes cast shall be necessary, save as otherwise provided by this Constitution.

Article 32

(1) The sessions of the National Council shall be open to the public.

(2) The public may be excluded upon request being made by the Chairman or by one-fifth of the members present and agreed to by the National Council after the withdrawal of the public.

Article 33

Truthful reports of the proceedings in the public sessions of the National Council and its committees shall be free from all liability.

II. The Federal Council

Article 34

(1) The Provinces shall be represented in the Federal Council in proportion to the number of citizens in each Province according to the following conditions.

(2) In regard to representation and status in the Federal Council, Vienna and the Province of Lower Austria (Articles 108 to 114) shall rank as independent Provinces.

(3) The Province having the largest number of citizens shall send twelve members and every other Province as many members as correspond to the ratio between the number of its citizens and the number of citizens in the first-mentioned Province, a remainder in excess of one-half the quota to count as a whole. Each Province shall, however, have a minimum repre-

sentation of three members. For each member a substitute shall be appointed.

Article 35

(1) The members of the Federal Council and their substitutes shall be elected by the Provincial Diets for the duration of their own legislative period according to the principles of proportional representation, but at least one seat must fall to the party having the second highest number of seats in the Provincial Diet or (if several parties have an equal number of seats) the second highest number of votes at the last election to the Provincial Diet. When the claims of several parties are equal, the matter shall be decided by lot.

(2) The members of the Federal Council shall not be members of the Provincial Diet which appoints them; they must, however, be eligible for election to that Diet.

(3) After the expiration of the legislative period of a Provincial Diet or after its dissolution, the members of the Federal Council appointed by it shall continue in office until the new Provincial Diet has carried out the election to the Federal Council.

(4) The provisions of this Article may be altered only when, in the Federal Council, the majority of representatives of at least four Provinces have accepted the alteration, apart from the majority of votes normally requisite for the passing of a measure in that body.

Article 36

(1) The Chairmanship of the Federal Council shall pass every six months to each of the different Provinces in turn, in alphabetical order.

(2) The office of Chairman shall be filled by the member sent up at the end of the list by the Province entitled to the Chairmanship for the time being: the appointment of substitute shall be regulated by the rules of procedure of the Federal Council.

(3) The Federal Council shall be summoned by its Chairman to meet at the seat of the National Council. The Chairman

shall be bound to summon the Federal Council immediately if so requested by at least one-fourth of its members or by the Federal Government.

Article 37

(1) Save as may be otherwise provided by this law, the presence of at least one-third of the members and an absolute majority of the votes cast shall be necessary to the taking of a valid decision by the Federal Council.

(2) The Federal Council shall determine its rules of procedure by resolution. For the adoption of this resolution the presence of one-half the members and a two-thirds' majority of the votes cast shall be necessary.

(3) The sessions of the Federal Council shall be public. The public may, however, be excluded by resolution in accordance with the rules of procedure. The provisions of Article 33 shall apply also to public sittings of the Federal Council and its Committees.

III. The Federal Assembly

Article 38

The National Council and the Federal Council shall meet as the Federal Assembly in joint public sitting, at the seat of the National Council, for the election of the President of the Federation and the taking of the oath by him, and also for decisions as to the declaration of war.

Article 39

(1) The Federal Assembly shall—apart from the cases mentioned in Article 63, paragraph 2, Article 64, paragraph 2, and Article 68, paragraph 2—be convened by the President of the Federation. The Chairmanship shall be assumed alternately by the Chairman of the National Council and the Chairman of the Federal Council, the former to assume the office in the first instance.

(2) The rules of procedure of the National Council shall be applied in principle in the Federal Assembly.

(3) The National Council and Federal Council may discuss the matter to be decided separately and in advance.

(4) The provisions of Article 33 shall also apply to sittings of the Federal Assembly.

Article 40

(1) Decisions of the Federal Assembly shall be authenticated by the Chairman and countersigned by the Federal Chancellor.

(2) The Federal Chancellor shall be responsible for the official promulgation of decisions.

IV. Methods of Federal Legislation

Article 41

(1) Legislation may be initiated in the National Council either by the members or by the Federal Government. The Federal Council may, through the medium of the Federal Government, bring proposals for legislation before the National Council.

(2) Any proposal for legislation (Popular Initiative Demand) supported by 200,000 voters or by half of the voters of three Provinces shall be introduced into the National Council by the Federal Government to be dealt with in accordance with the rules of procedure. The popular initiative demand must be expressed in the form of a draft bill.

Article 42

(1) Every law passed by the National Council shall be immediately transmitted by its Chairman to the Federal Chancellor, who shall communicate it at once to the Federal Council.

(2) A law shall, save as may be otherwise provided by Constitutional Law, be authenticated and promulgated only if the Federal Council agrees to it without amendment.

(3) Any proposed amendments must be communicated in writing to the National Council through the medium of the

Federal Chancellor within eight weeks after the law has been laid before the Federal Council.

(4) If the National Council reaffirms its original decision, at least half the members being present, the law as so reaffirmed shall be authenticated and promulgated. If the Federal Council accepts the law, or if no amendments are proposed within the period of time set out in paragraph 3, the law shall be authenticated and promulgated.

(5) The Federal Council may not amend laws passed by the National Council dealing with the rules of procedure of the National Council, the dissolution of the National Council, the granting of the Federal estimates, the ratification of the closing of accounts, the raising or conversion of Federal loans, or the administration of Federal property. Such laws passed by the National Council shall be authenticated and promulgated without further delay.

Article 43

Every law passed by the National Council shall be submitted to a Referendum before promulgation by the President of the Federation, if the National Council so decides or if the majority of the members of the National Council so request.

Article 44

(1) Constitutional laws or constitutional decisions incorporated in single laws require for their adoption by the National Council the presence of at least half of the members and a majority of two-thirds of the votes recorded; they shall be expressly designed as such ('Constitutional law', 'Constitutional decision').

(2) Every general alteration of the Constitution of the Federation and, if desired by one-third of the members of the National Council or of the Federal Council, every partial alteration thereof, shall be submitted to a vote of the whole people of the Federation, at the conclusion of the proceedings according to Article 42, and before promulgation by the President of the Federation.

Article 45

(1) The result of a Referendum shall be determined by an absolute majority of the validly recorded votes.

(2) The result of a Referendum shall be officially published.

Article 46

(1) The procedure in regard to the Popular Initiative Demand and the Referendum shall be regulated by Federal law.

(2) Every citizen of the Federation entitled to vote for the National Council shall be entitled to vote.

(3) The President of the Federation shall conduct the Referendum.

Article 47

(1) When Federal laws have been adopted in accordance with the Constitution, they shall be authenticated by the signature of the President of the Federation.

(2) The Federal Chancellor shall be responsible for the submission of documents for authentication by the President.

(3) The authentication shall be countersigned by the Federal Chancellor and by the competent Federal Ministers.

Article 48

Federal laws and the State treaties indicated in Article 50 shall be published subject to the decision of the National Council; Federal laws which are dependent on a Referendum shall be published subject to the result of the Referendum.

Article 49

(1) Federal laws and the State treaties indicated in Article 50 shall be published by the Federal Chancellor in the Federal Official Law Record. They shall come into force, if not otherwise expressly stated, at the expiration of the day of publication and dispatch of the part of the Federal Official Law Record in which they are published, and shall extend, if not otherwise expressly stated, over the whole Federation.

(2) The Federal Official Law Record shall be the subject of a special Federal law.

V. Co-operation of the National Council and the Federal Council in the Executive Administration of the Federation

Article 50

(1) All political State treaties and other treaties if they involve changes in the law require, to be valid, the approval of the National Council.

(2) The provisions of Article 42, paragraphs 1 to 4, and in cases when a Constitutional Law is altered by a State treaty, of Article 44, paragraph 1, shall be applied in principle to decisions of the National Council in relation to the approval of State treaties.

Article 51

An estimate of the income and expenditure of the Federation for the following financial year shall be laid before the National Council by the Federal Government at the latest eight weeks before the end of the financial year.

Article 52

The National Council and the Federal Council are authorized to investigate the conduct of business by the Federal Government, to question its members upon all matters relating to the execution of their duties, and to call for all information relating thereto, as well as to express, in the form of resolutions, their wishes with regard to the carrying out of their duties.

Article 53

(1) The National Council may by resolution set up Committees of Inquiry.

(2) The Courts of Justice and all other authorities shall be bound to comply with the requests of these Committees for the production of evidence; all public officials must produce official records when they are called for.

(3) The procedure of Committees of Inquiry shall be regulated by the law relating to the rules of procedure of the National Council.

Article 54

The National Council shall co-operate in fixing railway tariffs, post, telegraph, and telephone charges, and prices of monopolies, and in fixing the salaries of persons permanently employed in the service of the Federation. This co-operation shall be regulated by a Federal Constitutional Law.

Article 55

The National Council shall also co-operate in the executive administration of the Federation, in the cases specified by this law, through a Principal Committee elected from its members on the principle of proportional representation. It is especially incumbent on the Principal Committee to co-operate in the appointment of the Federal Government (Article 70). In addition, Federal legislation may prescribe that certain orders issued by the Federal Government shall be subject to agreement with the Principal Committee.

VI. Status of the Members of the National Council and of the Federal Council

Article 56

The members of the National Council and the members of the Federal Council shall not be bound by any instructions in the exercise of their functions.

Article 57

(1) Members of the National Council may not be made answerable for their votes given in the exercise of their office; and they shall be answerable only to the National Council for utterances made by them in the exercise of their office.

(2) No member of the National Council may be imprisoned or otherwise legally prosecuted for any penal offence—save when apprehended *flagrante delicto*—without the consent of the National Council.

(3) In the event of a member being apprehended *flagrante delicto*, the authorities must immediately notify the Chairman of the National Council of the arrest.

(4) If the National Council so demands, the arrest must be cancelled or the whole prosecution deferred for the duration of the legislative period.

(5) The immunity of the various organs of the National Council whose functions extend beyond the legislative period shall continue for the duration of their functions.

Article 58

The members of the Federal Council shall enjoy throughout their term of office the same immunity as members of the Diet which returned them.

Article 59

(1) No person may be a member at the same time of the National Council and of the Federal Council.

(2) Public employees, including those belonging to the Federal army, require no permission to be absent in order to act as members of the National Council or the Federal Council. If they become candidates for election to the National Council, the necessary free time shall be afforded them. Further provisions shall be laid down by the Service regulations.

THIRD SECTION

EXECUTIVE ADMINISTRATION OF THE FEDERATION

I. Administration

1. *President of the Federation*

Article 60

(1) The President of the Federation shall be elected by the Federal Assembly in acordance with Article 38 by secret ballot.

(2) His term of office shall be four years. Re-election for the term of office immediately following is permissible on only one occasion.

(3) Only persons who are entitled to vote for the National Council and who have passed their thirty-fifth year on 1 January in the year of election, may be elected as President of the Federation.

(4) Members of reigning houses, or of such families as have formerly reigned, are not eligible for election.

(5) The person in whose favour more than one-half of all the votes recorded are cast shall be elected. The balloting shall be repeated until there is an absolute majority for one person.

Article 61

The President of the Federation may not during his period of office belong to any public representative body nor follow any other calling.

Article 62

The President of the Federation on entering into office shall give his solemn undertaking before the Federal Assembly:

"I solemnly promise that I will faithfully observe the Constitution and all the laws of the Republic, and do my duty to the best of my knowledge and conscience."

Article 63

(1) Legal proceedings may be taken against the President of the Federation only by decision of the Federal Assembly.

(2) A motion to institute legal proceedings against the President of the Federation shall be submitted by the competent authorities to the National Council, which shall decide whether the matter is to be brought before the Federal Assembly. If the National Council so decides, the Federal Chancellor shall immediately call together the Federal Assembly.

Article 64

(1) When the President of the Federation is unable to perform his duties or when his position becomes permanently

vacant, all the functions of the President of the Federation are transferred to the Federal Chancellor.

(2) In the case of the permanent vacancy of the position of President of the Federation, the Federal Chancellor shall immediately call together the Federal Assembly for the election of a new President of the Federation.

Article 65

(1) The President of the Federation shall represent the Republic in its external relations, receive and accredit ambassadors, accord recognition to foreign consuls, appoint the consular representatives of the Republic abroad, and conclude State treaties.

(2) Further—in addition to the powers conferred upon him by other provisions of this Constitution—he shall fulfil the following functions:

a. The appointment of Federal officials, including army officers, and other Federal functionaries; the granting of official titles to such;
b. The creation and granting of professional titles;
c. In individual cases: the pardoning of persons lawfully sentenced by the Courts, the mitigation and alteration of penalties inflicted by the Courts, the postponement of the execution of sentences and the annulment of sentences as an act of mercy, and the quashing of judicial proceedings in regard to offences committed in the exercise of official authority;
d. The declaring of illegitimate children as legitimate on the application of the parents.

(3) Special laws shall determine the extent to which the President of the Federation may exercise further powers with regard to the granting of honorary rights, extraordinary grants, extra allowances and maintenance allowances, rights of appointment and confirmation, and other powers in regard to personal matters.

Article 66

(1) The President of the Federation may transfer his right

of appointing Federal employees of certain categories to the competent members of the Federal Government.

(2) The President of the Federation may authorize the Federal Government or the competent members of the Federal Government to conclude certain categories of State treaties which do not come under the provisions of Article 50.

Article 67

(1) All acts of the President of the Federation, save as may be otherwise provided in accordance with the Constitution, shall be done on the initiative of the Federal Government or of the Federal Ministers empowered by it. The extent to which the Federal Government or the competent Federal Ministers shall be themselves bound by proposals from other authorities shall be defined by law.

(2) All acts of the President of the Federation require, in order to be valid, the counter-signature of the Federal Chancellor or the competent Federal Minister.

Article 68

(1) The President of the Federation shall be responsible for the discharge of his duties to the Federal Assembly in conformity with Article 142.

(2) For the purpose of enforcing this responsibility, the Federal Assembly shall be called together by the Federal Chancellor at the demand of the National Council or of the Federal Council.

(3) The adoption of a resolution of impeachment within the meaning of Article 142 requires the presence of more than one-half of the members of each of the two representative bodies and a majority of two-thirds of the votes recorded.

2. *The Federal Government*

Article 69

(1) The Federal Chancellor, the Vice-Chancellor, and the other Federal Ministers shall be entrusted with the highest administrative offices of the Federation, in so far as these are

not entrusted to the President of the Federation. Collectively, they constitute the Federal Government under the presidency of the Federal Chancellor.

(2) The Vice-Chancellor shall be appointed to act as substitute for the Federal Chancellor in respect of all his functions.

Article 70

(1) The Federal Government shall be elected as a whole by the National Council, by poll of the members by name, on a motion to be submitted by the Principal Committee.

(2) Only persons who are eligible for the National Council may be elected to the Federal Government; the members of the Federal Government must not belong to the National Council.

(3) If the National Council is not in session, the Federal Government shall be appointed provisionally by the Principal Committee; as soon as the National Council meets, the election shall take place.

(4) The provisions of paragraphs 1 to 3 shall be applied in principle to the appointment of individual members of the Federal Government.

Article 71

When the Federal Government goes out of office, the President of the Federation shall, until the new Federal Government is formed, entrust the carrying on of the administration to members of the outgoing Government or to higher officials of the Federal Departments, and shall appoint one of them as President of the Provisional Federal Government. This provision shall be applied in principle when individual members of the Federal Government go out of office.

Article 72

(1) The members of the Federal Government, before taking up office, shall be sworn in by the President of the Federation.

(2) The warrants of appointment of the Federal Chancellor, the Vice-Chancellor, and the other Federal Ministers shall be completed by the President of the Federation by the day on

which they are sworn in and countersigned by the newly appointed Federal Chancellor.

(3) The principle of these provisions shall also be applied to cases coming under Article 71.

Article 73

In the event of a Federal Minister being temporarily unable to discharge his duties, the President of the Federation shall appoint one of the Federal Ministers or a higher official of a Federal Department as a substitute for him. This substitute shall bear the same responsibility as a Federal Minister (Article 76).

Article 74

(1) If the National Council by express resolution withdraws its confidence from the Federal Government or from any individual member thereof, the Federal Government or the Federal Minister in question shall be removed from office.

(2) For the adoption by the National Council of a resolution withdrawing confidence, the presence of one-half the members of the National Council shall be requisite. Even so, upon demand by one-fifth of the members present, the voting may be deferred to the next working-day but one. Any further adjournment of the voting may take place only by decision of the National Council.

(3) The Federal Government and its individual members shall be relieved of their office by the President of the Federation in the cases prescribed by law or at their own request.

Article 75

The members of the Federal Government and also the substitutes appointed by them are entitled to participate in all deliberations of the National Council, the Federal Council, and the Federal Assembly, and of the committees connected with those representative bodies, and if specially invited by the Committee, in the deliberations of the Principal Committee of the National Council. They must be heard whenever they so demand. The National Council, the Federal Council, and the

Federal Assembly, as well as their Committees, may require the attendance of members of the Federal Government.

Article 76

(1) The members of the Federal Government (Articles 69 and 71) shall be responsible to the National Council, in accordance with Article 142.

(2) For the adoption of a resolution of impeachment in accordance with the terms of Article 142, the presence of more than one-half the members shall be requisite.

Article 77

(1) The administrative business of the Federation shall be conducted by the Federal Ministries and the Departments subordinate to them.

(2) The number of Federal Ministries, their sphere of action, and their organization shall be determined by Federal law.

(3) The Federal Chancellor shall be responsible for the control of the Federal Chancellory, and each of the Federal Ministers shall be responsible for the control of another Federal Ministry.

(4) The Federal Chancellor and the other Federal Ministers may, under exceptional circumstances, be entrusted also with the control of a second Federal Ministry.

Article 78

(1) In special cases a Federal Minister may be appointed without being simultaneously entrusted with the control of a Federal Ministry.

(2) Secretaries of State may be appointed to assist Federal Ministers in their administrative and parliamentary duties; they shall be appointed to and shall retire from office in the same manner as the Federal Ministers.

(3) A Secretary of State shall be subordinate to the Federal Minister and shall be bound by his instructions.

3. *The Federal Army*

Article 79

(1) The protection of the frontiers of the Republic is the duty of the Federal Army.

(2) The Federal Army may be employed, in so far as the legitimate civil authority requests its co-operation, to protect the institutions established under the Constitution, to maintain order and security in the interior generally, and to afford assistance in natural occurrences and disasters of unusual extent.

Article 80

(1) The National Council shall have control over the Army. In so far as direct control is not reserved to the National Council by the Army Law, the Federal Government, or the competent Federal Minister within the limits of the authority conferred upon him by the Federal Government, shall be responsible for the control of the Army.

(2) The Army Law shall determine the extent to which the authorities of the Provinces and the Communes may avail themselves directly of the co-operation of the Federal Army for the purposes mentioned in Article 79, paragraph 2.

Article 81

The extent to which the Provinces shall co-operate in the recruitment, provisioning, and housing of the Army, and in supplying its needs in other respects, shall be determined by Federal legislation.

II. Judicial Power

Article 82

(1) All judicial power emanates from the Federation.

(2) Judgements and verdicts shall be given and executed in the name of the Republic.

Article 83

(1) The constitution and jurisdiction of the courts of law shall be determined by Federal law.

(2) No person may be withdrawn from his ordinary judge.

(3) Extraordinary courts are only permissible in the cases determined by the laws on procedure in criminal matters.

Article 84

Military jurisdiction is abolished, except in times of war.

Article 85

The death penalty in ordinary procedure is abolished.

Article 86

(1) Save as otherwise provided by this law, the judges shall be appointed, on the nomination of the Federal Government, by the President of the Federation, or, under his authorization, by the competent Federal Minister; the Federal Government or the Federal Minister shall receive nominations for appointment from the Senates appointed for the purpose under the Judiciary Law.

(2) The nominations for appointment to be laid before the competent Federal Minister and transmitted by him to the Federal Government must, if sufficient applications are available, include at least three persons, or, if more than one position is to be filled, at least twice as many persons as there are judges to be appointed.

Article 87

(1) Judges shall be independent in the exercise of their judicial functions.

(2) In the exercise of his judicial office, a judge must be prepared to discharge all business, excluding administrative matters, which is allotted to him in the distribution of judicial business in accordance with the law and which is not required by law to be dealt with by Senates or Commissions.

(3) The distribution of business among the judges of each Court shall be determined in advance for a period fixed by the Judiciary Law. A case allotted to a judge in accordance with this distribution may be withdrawn from him by order of the judicial administration only in the event of his inability to act.

Article 88

(1) An age limit shall be fixed by the Judiciary Law, after the attainment of which the judges shall be permanently retired from office.

(2) Save as aforesaid, judges may be removed from office, or transferred against their will to another post, or retired from office, only in the cases and in the manner prescribed by law and in pursuance of a formal judicial decision. These conditions do not, however, apply to transfers or retirements necessitated by changes in the organization of the Courts. In such cases the period within which judges may be transferred or retired without the prescribed formalities shall be determined by law.

(3) The temporary removal of judges from office may take place only by order of the President of the Court or of the higher judicial authority, the matter being at the same time referred to the competent Court.

Article 89

(1) The Courts may not inquire into the validity of any duly promulgated law.

(2) If a Court has any doubt as to the applicability of a decree on the ground of conflict with the law, the proceedings must be discontinued and an application made to the Constitutional Court for the cancellation of the decree.

Article 90

(1) Proceedings before Courts in which criminal and civil cases are decided must be conducted orally and in public. Exceptions to this rule shall be determined by law.

(2) Criminal proceedings shall be by indictment.

Article 91

(1) The people shall co-operate in the administration of justice.

(2) In the case of offences punishable with heavy penalties specified by law, as also in all political crimes and offences, the guilt of the accused shall be decided by a jury.

(3) In criminal proceedings relative to other penal offences, Assessors shall participate in the administration of justice if the penalty to be inflicted exceeds a limit to be determined by law.

Article 92

The Supreme Court of Justice in Vienna shall be the court of final appeal in civil and criminal cases.

Article 93

Amnesties for actions punishable by law may be granted by Federal law.

Article 94

(1) Judicial proceedings shall be kept separate in all stages from administrative legal proceedings.

(2) When an administrative authority has to decide upon claims under the Civil Law, any person who deems himself injured by the decision may, save as otherwise provided by law, seek a remedy against the other party through the ordinary legal channels.

(3) In matters connected with land reform (Article 12, paragraph 1 f) the right of decision is reserved exclusively to Commissions composed of judges, administrative officials, and experts.

FOURTH SECTION

LEGISLATION AND EXECUTIVE ADMINISTRATION OF PROVINCES

I. General Provisions

Article 95

(1) The legislative powers of the Provinces shall be exercised by the Provincial Diets. The members of these shall be elected by the equal, direct, secret, personal and proportional suffrage of all male and female Federal citizens who are entitled to vote

in accordance with the electoral ordinances of the Provincial Diet, and have their ordinary domicile in the Province.

(2) The electoral ordinances of the Provincial Diet may not restrict the active and passive electoral right more narrowly than the electoral ordinance for the National Council.

(3) The electors shall exercise their right to vote in electoral districts, each of which must comprise a self-contained area. The number of representatives for each electoral district shall be proportionate to the number of citizens. The electorate may not be split up into other electoral bodies.

Article 96

(1) The members of a Provincial Diet shall enjoy the same privilege of immunity as the members of the National Council; the principles of the provisions of Article 57 shall be applicable to them.

(2) The provisions of Articles 32 and 33 shall also apply to the sessions of the Provincial Diets and their Committees.

Article 97

(1) Every Provincial law must be adopted by the Provincial Diet, authenticated and countersigned in accordance with the requirements of the Provincial Constitution, and finally promulgated by the Provincial Governor in the Official Record of Provincial Laws (*Landesgesetzblatt*).

(2) In so far as a Provincial law provides for the co-operation of the Federal authorities in its execution, the consent of the Federal Government must be obtained for that co-operation. Until such consent is obtained, the Provincial law may not be promulgated.

Article 98

(1) The adoption of a law by the Provincial Diet must be communicated immediately after such adoption to the competent Federal Ministry before being sanctioned by the Governor of the Province.

(2) The Federal Government may, on the ground of danger to the interests of the Federation, enter an objection, supported

by reasons, against the adoption of the law, within eight weeks from the day on which that adoption was communicated to the competent Federal Minister. In such a case, the law may be promulgated only if it is reaffirmed by the Provincial Diet, at least one-half of its members being present.

(3) Promulgation before the expiration of the period allowed for lodging objections shall be permissible only if the Federal Government expressly agrees thereto.

Article 99

(1) The Provincial Constitution, which shall be decreed by Provincial law, may be altered by Provincial law, in so far as the Federal Constitution is not affected thereby.

(2) A Provincial Constitution law shall require for its adoption the presence of one-half the members of the Provincial Diet and a majority of two-thirds of the votes cast.

Article 100

(1) Each Provincial Diet may be dissolved by the President of the Federation, on the motion of the Federal Government and with the assent of the Federal Council. The assent of the Federal Council shall require the presence of one-half of its members and a majority of two-thirds of the votes cast. The representatives of the Provincial Diet about to be dissolved may not take part in the voting.

(2) In the event of dissolution, fresh elections must be announced within three weeks, in accordance with the terms of the Provincial Constitution; the newly elected Provincial Diet must be summoned within four weeks of the election.

Article 101

(1) The executive administration of each Province shall be carried on by the Provincial Government elected by the Provincial Diet.

(2) The members of the Provincial Government shall not be members of the Provincial Diet. Nevertheless, no person may be elected to the Provincial Government unless he be qualified for election to the Provincial Diet.

(3) The Provincial Government shall consist of the Governor of the Province, the requisite number of substitutes, and further members.

(4) Before entering into office, the Governor of the Province shall be sworn in by the President of the Federation, and the other members of the Provincial Government by the Governor of the Province.

Article 102

(1) The Federal executive administration within the territories of the Provinces shall, save where there are special Federal authorities (direct Federal administration), be carried out by the Governor of the Province and the Provincial authorities subordinate to him (indirect Federal administration).

(2) The following matters may be dealt with directly by Federal authorities within the limits of their spheres of action as laid down in accordance with the Constitution:

Defining of boundaries, foreign trade in goods and live stock, customs, Federal finances, monopolies, weights, measures, standards and gauges, technical experiments, justice, matters of trade and industry, patents, trade marks, patterns and other distinctive markings of goods, engineering and civil technology, transport, Federal roads, river and ship police, posts, telegraphs and telephones, mining, regulation and conservation of waters, construction and upkeep of waterways, hydrographic service, land surveying, labour laws, protection of labourers and employees, social insurance, protection of monuments, Federal police, Federal gendarmerie, military matters, care of persons who have served in the war and of their dependants.

(3) The Federation may entrust the Federal executive administration to the Governor of a Province, even in regard to the matters set out in paragraph (2).

(4) Special Federal authorities for matters other than those set out in paragraph (2) may be established only with the assent of the Provinces concerned.

(5) The extent to which the Governors of Provinces shall have control of the Federal police and Federal gendarmerie

shall be regulated by the Federal legislation referred to in Article 120, paragraph (1).

Article 103

In matters of indirect Federal administration the Governor of the Province shall be bound by the instructions of the Federal Government and of the various Federal Ministers; in these matters, administrative appeals may be carried up to the competent Federal Ministers, unless otherwise expressly provided by Federal law.

Article 104

The conditions of Article 122 shall not be applicable to the arrangements for transacting Federal affairs in matters specified in Article 17.

Article 105

(1) The Governor of the Province shall represent the Province. In matters of indirect Federal administration he shall be responsible to the Federal Government, in accordance with Article 142. No immunity shall constitute any bar to the enforcement of this responsibility.

(2) The members of the Provincial Government shall be responsible to the Provincial Diet in accordance with Article 142.

(3) For the adoption of a resolution of impeachment within the meaning of Article 142, the presence of one-half the members shall be necessary.

Article 106

An administrative official versed in the law shall be appointed as Director of the Provincial Administration, to direct the internal administration of the Provincial Government. He shall also assist the Governor of the Province in matters of indirect Federal administration.

Article 107

Provinces may take joint action with one another only in

matters coming within their sphere of independent action, and such action must at once be reported to the Federal Government.

II. The Federal Capital, Vienna, and the Province of Lower Austria

Article 108

(1) The Provincial Diet of Lower Austria shall be divided into two Assemblies (Curiae). One of these (the Provincial Assembly) shall consist of the Deputies of the Province excluding those representing Vienna. The election of the other (the City Assembly) shall be regulated by the Constitution of the Federal Capital, Vienna.

(2) The number of Deputies to be allotted to each of the two Assemblies shall be proportionate to the number of citizens.

Article 109

Both the Assemblies shall meet together as the Provincial Diet of Lower Austria for the purpose of legislating on all matters connected with the former autonomous Provincial administration declared by the Provincial Constitution to be of common concern, including, in particular, the common Constitution of the Province.

Article 110

(1) In matters which are not of common concern, each of the two divisions of the Province shall have the status of an independent Province.

(2) In such matters the Municipal Council of Vienna and the Provincial Assembly shall function as Provincial Diets for Vienna and for the Province of Lower Austria respectively. The principles of Article 57 shall be applicable to the members of the Municipal Council of Vienna.

Article 111

(1) The Constitution of each of the two divisions of the

Province and the election of members of the Federal Council shall be deemed to be matters which are not of common concern (Article 35).

(2) Similarly, legislation relating to taxation, in so far as it falls within the sphere of action of the Province, shall devolve upon the Municipal Council of the City of Vienna and on the Provincial Diet (Provincial Assembly).

(3) The raising of money for matters of common concern shall be governed by the common Constitution of the Province.

Article 112

The general provisions of this Section shall apply to both divisions of the Province. In Vienna, accordingly, the Burgomaster elected by the Municipal Council shall function as the Governor of a Province, the City Senate elected by the Municipal Council shall function as the Provincial Government, and the Magistrate-Director shall function as the Director of Provincial Administration.

Article 113

(1) Matters of common concern shall be administered by an Administrative Commission to be elected by the Provincial Diet from among its members by proportional representation.

(2) The Burgomaster of the City of Vienna and the Governor of the Province of Lower Austria shall be members of the Administrative Commission, and shall preside over it alternately.

Article 114

Vienna may be constituted a separate Province by laws passed in identical terms by the Municipal Council of Vienna and by the Diet of the Province of Lower Austria.

III. Communes

Article 115

The general State Administration in the Provinces shall be organized according to the following provisions on the basis of self-government.

Article 116

(1) The administrative districts and self-governing areas into which the Provinces shall be divided shall consist of Local Communes and District Communes.

(2) The Local Communes shall be subordinate to the District Communes and the latter to the Provinces.

Article 117

(1) Local Communes with more than 20,000 inhabitants shall, if they so desire, be declared to be District Communes. In the case of such Communes the circuit administration (*Bezirksverwaltung*) shall coincide with the communal administration.

(2) Urban districts hitherto organized as towns with their own charters shall become District Communes.

Article 118

The Local Communes and District Communes shall also be independent economic corporations; they shall be entitled to hold and acquire property of all kinds and to dispose of it within the limits prescribed by Federal and Provincial laws, to carry on economic undertakings, to manage their own finances, and to levy taxes.

Article 119

(1) The public authorities of the Local Communes shall be the Local Communal Representative Council and the Local Communal Administration; the public authorities of the District Communes shall be the District Communal Representative Council and the District Communal Administration.

(2) Elections to all representative councils shall be by equal, direct, secret, personal and proportional suffrage of all Federal citizens ordinarily domiciled in the area of the representative council. Regulations as to the elections shall be prescribed by Provincial legislation; the active and passive electoral rights of citizens may not be more narrowly restricted by these regulations than is the case for the elections to the National Council. The electoral regulations may provide that electors

shall exercise their electoral rights in electoral districts, each of which must be self-contained. No division of the electorate into other electoral bodies shall be permitted. The Judicial Circuit District shall constitute the electoral district for elections to the District Communal Representative Council. The number of representatives to be allotted to each electoral district shall be proportionate to the number of citizens.

(3) Only persons who are ordinarily domiciled within the area of the District Commune and who are eligible for election to the Provincial Diet shall be eligible to the District Communal Representative Council.

(4) The Councils may appoint from among their own number, on the basis of proportional representation, special administrative committees for the individual branches of the administration: and these committees may, when certain occupational groups or groups with special interests are under consideration, add representatives of such groups to their numbers.

(5) The directors of the District Communal Administrations must be administrative officials versed in the law.

Article 120

(1) The establishment of further principles for the organization of the general State administration in the Provinces according to Articles 115–119 shall be effected by Federal Constitutional laws; the application of these principles shall be effected by Provincial laws.

(2) The allocation of administrative affairs, to be dealt with directly or by way of appeal, between the Representative Councils, the Administrative Committees, and the Administrations, shall be determined by Federal and Provincial legislation within the limits of their respective constitutional competence.

(3) The Local Communes shall, notwithstanding the foregoing provision, be competent to deal in the first instance with the following matters:

a. Measures for the protection of person and property (Local Security Police);
b. Relief and life-saving services;

c. Measures for the upkeep of roads, streets, public places, and bridges in the Commune;
d. Local street police services;
e. Rural police services;
f. Market and food control police services;
g. Sanitary police services;
h. Building and fire police services.

FIFTH SECTION

CONTROL OF FEDERAL ACCOUNTS

Article 121

(1) The auditing of the administration of the general State finances of the Federation and of the administration of foundations, funds, and institutions administered by Federal authorities shall be conducted by the Court of Accounts. The auditing of the administration of enterprises in which the Federation is financially interested may also be entrusted to the Court of Accounts.

(2) The Court of Accounts shall prepare the final statement of Accounts of the Federation and lay it before the National Council.

(3) All documents relating to State debts (financial and administrative liabilities) shall, if they involve any obligation on the Federation, be countersigned by the President of the Court of Accounts; the legality and correct accountancy of the administration merely shall be vouched for by this countersignature.

Article 122

(1) The Court of Accounts shall be directly subordinate to the National Council.

(2) The Court of Accounts shall consist of a President and the requisite officials and assistants.

(3) The President of the Court of Accounts shall be elected

on the motion of the Principal Committee of the National Council.

(4) The President of the Court of Accounts may not be a member of any public representative body, nor may he have been a member of the Federal Government or of a Provincial Government within the last five years.

Article 123

(1) The President of the Court of Accounts shall be answerable for the discharge of his duties on the same basis as members of the Federal Government.

(2) He may be removed from office by resolution of the National Council.

Article 124

(1) The official next in rank to the President of the Court of Accounts shall act as deputy for him.

(2) Where a deputy is acting for the President, the provisions of Article 123 shall apply to the deputy.

Article 125

(1) The officials of the Court of Accounts shall be appointed by the President of the Federation on the proposition and with the counter-signature of the President of the Court of Accounts; this provision shall apply also to the conferring of official titles. The President of the Federation may, nevertheless, empower the President of the Court of Accounts to appoint certain classes of officials.

(2) Assistants shall be appointed by the President of the Court of Accounts.

Article 126

No member of the Court of Accounts may take part in the direction or administration of enterprises which have to render account to the Federation or to the Provinces or which are in receipt of a subsidy from or under contract to the Federation or the Provinces. This provision shall not apply to enterprises devoted to humanitarian purposes, or concerned with the economic position of public officials or their dependants.

Article 127

Provincial Constitutional laws may transfer to the Court of Accounts duties relating to the administration of the Provinces which are similar to the duties relating to the administration of the Federation which are entrusted to the Court by this law.

Article 128

Further provisions as to the functions of the Court of Accounts shall be prescribed by Federal legislation.

SIXTH SECTION

CONSTITUTIONAL AND ADMINISTRATIVE GUARANTEES

I. The Administrative Court

Article 129

(1) Any person claiming that his rights have been impaired by an illegal decision or decree of an administrative authority may, after carrying the matter through all the stages of administrative appeal, lodge a complaint with the Administrative Court.

(2) If the competent Federal Minister is of opinion that the interests of the Federation in matters specified in Articles 11 and 12 have been prejudiced by an illegal decision or decree of a Provincial authority, he may in the name of the Federation lodge a complaint of infringement of the law with the Administrative Court.

(3) No action for infringement of the law shall lie in any case where the authority is accorded, by the provisions of the law, free discretion as to the decision or decree and has exercised that discretion within the meaning of the law.

Article 130

In respect of matters in which a complaint may be lodged with the Administrative Court, the process of administrative appeal may be shortened by legislation by the Federation or by the Provinces as may be appropriate in accordance with Articles 10–15.

Article 131

The following matters are excluded from the jurisdiction of the Administrative Court:

(1) Matters falling within the jurisdiction of the Constitutional Court;

(2) Matters upon which the ordinary Courts are competent to decide;

(3) Matters which must be heard or decided by a joint Board (*Kollegialbehörde*), of which at least one member, in the first or later stages, must be a judge.

Article 132

A judge who has passed through the judicial or administrative service in the Province concerned shall normally be a member of any division of the Administrative Court which has to give judgement upon a disputed decision or decree of a Provincial authority.

Article 133

(1) An illegal decision or decree shall be cancelled upon judgement to that effect being given by the Administrative Court.

(2) The administrative authorities shall be bound in the issue of a new decision or decree by the legal opinion expressed by the Administrative Court.

(3) The Administrative Court may itself decide the action to be taken in any case, provided that the matter is not one which, in accordance with the provisions of the law, is left to the free discretion of the authorities.

Article 134

(1) The seat of the Administrative Court shall be in the Federal Capital, Vienna.

(2) It shall consist of a President, a Vice-President, and the requisite number of presidents of divisions and councillors.

(3) At least half of the members must possess the qualifications required for holding office as a judge.

Article 135

The President, Vice-President, and the members of the Administrative Court shall be appointed by the President of the Federation on the nomination of the Federal Government. As regards the President and one-half the members of the Court, the nominations made by the Federal Government must have the assent of the Principal Committee of the National Council; as regards the Vice-President and the other half of the members, the nominations must have the assent of the Federal Council.

Article 136

The administrative jurisdiction and the organization of the Administrative Court shall be determined by Federal Law.

II. The Constitutional Court

Article 137

The Constitutional Court shall give judgement upon all claims made upon the Federation, the Provinces, or the Communes, which cannot be decided by the ordinary judicial procedure.

Article 138

The Constitutional Court shall also have jurisdiction in all disputes as to competence:

(1) between the Courts and Administrative authorities;

(2) between the Administrative Court and the ordinary Courts, and more especially between the Administrative Court and the Constitutional Court itself.

(3) between Provinces and also between a Province and the Federation.

Article 139

(1) The Constitutional Court shall give judgement as to the illegality of orders issued by any Federal or Provincial authority upon the motion of a Court, or, *ex officio*, when the order presupposes a finding by the Constitutional Court, and also on the motion of the Federal Government in regard to the illegality of orders issued by a Provincial Government, and on the motion of a Provincial Government in regard to the illegality of orders issued by the Federal Government.

(2) Immediately upon judgement being given by the Constitutional Court annulling an order as illegal, the competent authority shall publish notice of the annulment, which shall take effect from the day of publication.

Article 140

(1) The Constitutional Court shall give judgement in all questions as to the unconstitutionality of laws, in the case of Provincial laws upon the motion of the Federal Government, and in the case of Federal laws upon the motion of a Provincial Government, but *ex officio* when the law presupposes a finding by the Constitutional Court.

(2) The motion mentioned in paragraph (1) may be brought forward at any time; the authority responsible for the motion must immediately communicate it to the Provincial Government concerned or to the Federal Government.

(3) Immediately upon delivery of a judgement by the Constitutional Court annulling a law as unconstitutional, the Federal Chancellor or the Governor of the Province concerned shall publish notice of the annulment, which shall take effect from the day of publication unless the Constitutional Court fixes a period for the annulment. This period may not exceed six months.

(4) The provision of Article 89, paragraph (1), shall not apply to an inquiry into the constitutionality of laws by the Constitutional Court.

Article 141

The Constitutional Court shall give judgement upon cases of disputed elections to the National Council, the Federal Council, the Provincial Diets and all other public representative bodies and, on the motion of any such representative body, upon a declaration of forfeiture of a seat by one of its members.

Article 142

(1) The Constitutional Court shall give judgement upon motions of impeachment of the supreme Federal and Provincial authorities for illegal acts committed in the exercise of their official functions.

(2) The motion of impeachment may be made:

a. When directed against the Federal President, on the ground of violation of the Federal Constitution—by decision of the Federal Assembly;
b. When directed against members of the Federal Government and authorities subject to the same constitutional responsibility in relation to them, on the ground of violation of the law—by decision of the National Council;
c. When directed against members of a Provincial Government and authorities subjected to the same responsibility by the Provincial Constitution, on the ground of violation of the law—by decision of the Provincial Diet concerned;
d. When directed against the Governor of a Province, on the ground of violation of the law or failure to comply with the decrees or other instructions of the Federation in matters of indirect Federal administration—by decision of the Federal Government.

(3) An adverse finding by the Constitutional Court shall involve removal from office, and also, in exceptionally grave cases, deprivation of political rights for a period; in respect of minor infringements of the law in the cases referred to in paragraph (2), section d, the Constitutional Court may confine itself to establishing the fact of a breach of the law.

Article 143

Proceedings against the persons mentioned in Article 142

may also be instituted in respect of a criminal offence committed in the execution of official duties. In such cases the Constitutional Court shall have exclusive jurisdiction; any proceedings which may be pending in the ordinary Criminal Courts shall be transferred to the Constitutional Court. The Constitutional Court may in such cases apply the provisions of the penal law in addition to those of Article 142, paragraph (3).

Article 144

(1) The Constitutional Court shall give judgement on complaints of violation, by a decision or decree of an administrative authority, of rights guaranteed under the Constitution, after the matter has been taken through all the stages of administrative appeal.

(2) An unconstitutional decision or decree shall be annulled on judgement to that effect being given by the Constitutional Court. The authorities shall be bound by the legal opinion expressed by the Constitutional Court in the issue of any new decision or decree.

Article 145

The Constitutional Court shall give judgement upon violations of international law in accordance with the provision of a special Federal law.

Article 146

The Federal President shall be responsible for the execution of the judgements of the Constitutional Court.

Article 147

(1) The Constitutional Court shall sit in Vienna.

(2) It shall consist of a President, a Vice-President, and the requisite number of members and substitute members.

(3) The President, Vice-President, and one-half of the members and deputy members shall be elected by the National Council, and the other half of the members and deputy members by the Federal Council, and they shall hold office for life.

Article 148

Further provisions as to the organization and procedure of the Constitutional Court shall be prescribed by Federal legislation.

SEVENTH SECTION

FINAL PROVISIONS

Article 149

(1) In addition to this Law, the following enactments shall be deemed to be Constitutional Laws within the meaning of Article 44, paragraph (1), subject to the alterations provided for by this Law:

Law of 21 December 1867, *Reichsgesetzblatt*[1] No. 142, on the public rights of State citizens for the Kingdoms and Provinces represented in the *Reichsrat*.

Law of 27 October 1862, R. G. Bl. No. 87, on the protection of personal liberty.

Law of 27 October 1862, R. G. Bl. No. 88, on the protection of domiciliary rights.

Decree of the Provisional National Assembly of 30 October 1918, St. G. Bl. No. 3 (*Staatsgesetzblatt* No. 3).

Law of 3 April 1919, St. G. Bl. No. 209, concerning the banishment and the taking over of the property of the House of Habsburg-Lorraine.

Law of 3 April 1919, St. G. Bl. No. 211, relating to the abolition of the nobility, the temporal orders of Knights and Dames, and certain titles and dignities.

Law of 8 May 1919, St. G. Bl. No. 257, relating to the State arms and State seal of the Republic of German Austria, with the alterations effected by Articles 2, 5, and 6 of the Law of 21 October 1919, St. G. Bl. No. 484.

Section V of Part III of the Treaty of St. Germain of 10 September 1919, St. G. Bl. No. 303, of 1920.[2]

(2) Article 20 of the Law of 21 December 1867, R. G. Bl.

[1] The official collection of laws.

[2] This section comprises the stipulations as to protection of minorities imposed upon Austria by the Allied and Associated Powers.

No. 142, and the Law of 5 May 1869, R. G. Bl. No. 66, based upon that Article, are repealed.

Article 150

The transition to the Federal Constitution established by this Law shall be regulated by a separate Constitutional law which shall come into operation simultaneously with this Law.

Article 151

(1) This Law shall come into operation on the day of the first sitting of the National Council, save in so far as exceptions may be made by the Law mentioned in Article 150.

(2) Nevertheless the provisions of Article 50, paragraph (1), and of Article 66, paragraph (2), shall come into force on the day of the promulgation, the right of approval vested in the National Council being exercised by the National Assembly until the coming into operation of the other provisions of this Law.

Article 152

The State Government is entrusted with the execution of this Law.

APPENDIX C

Austrian Governments, 1918–34

15 March 1919 to 17 October 1919, Renner. Coalition of Social Democrats and Christian Socialists.

17 October 1919 to 7 July 1920, Mayr. Coalition of Christian Socialists and Social Democrats.

7 July 1920 to 10 November 1920, 'Proporz' Cabinet.

10 November 1920 to 21 May 1921, Mayr. Christian Socialists.

21 July 1921 to 24 May 1922, Schober. Officials and Christian Socialists.

24 May 1922 to 8 November 1924, Seipel. Christian Socialists.

18 November 1924 to 15 October 1925, Ramek. Christian Socialists.

26 October 1925 to 4 March 1927, Seipel. Christian Socialists.

19 March 1927 to 3 April 1929, Seipel. Christian Socialists.

5 May 1929 to 25 September 1929, Steeruwitz. Christian Socialists.

26 September 1929 to 28 September 1930, Schober. Christian Socialists and Officials.

28 September 1930 to 30 November 1930, Vaugoin. Clericals and *Heimwehr*.

3 December 1930 to 12 June 1931, Ender. Christian Socialists.

18 June 1931 to 20 June 1921, Seipel. Christian Socialists.

21 June 1931 to 20 May 1932, Buresch. Christian Socialists.

20 May 1932 to 25 July 1934, Dollfuss. Christian Socialists.

Note. The German Nationalists as a rule supported the Christian Socialists.

BIBLIOGRAPHY

Books of particular value, either by reason of their authorship or their contents, are indicated by an asterisk.

I. General Historical Sources

Bulletin of International News. Royal Institute of International Affairs. Issued fortnightly.

Bundesgesetzblatt für die Republik Österreich.

League of Nations. *Official Journal.*

League of Nations. *Treaty Series.*

Staatsgesetzblatt für den Staat Deutschösterreich.

Stenographische Protokolle über die Sitzungen der provisorischen Nationalversammlung für Deutschösterreich, u. Beilage. 1918–19.

Stenographische Protokolle über die Sitzungen der konstituirenden Nationalversammlung der Republik Österreich, u. Beilage. 1919.

Stenographische Protokolle über die Sitzungen der Nationalversammlung, u. Beilage. 1920.

Survey of International Affairs, ed. A. J. Toynbee. Oxford University Press for Royal Institute of International Affairs. Annual volumes, 1920–34.

II. Constitutional History

Adamovich. *Österreichisches Verfassungsrecht.* Mit der Verfassungsreform des Jahres, 1925. Wien u. Leipzig, 1923.

Die österreichischen Verfassungsgesetze des Bundes, samt Ausführungs —u. Nebengesetzen. Adamovich, Ludwig and Froelich (editors), 2nd edition. Wien. Österreichische Staatsdruckerei, 1932.

*Kelsen, Hans. *Die Verfassungsgesetze der Republik Deutschösterreich.* Wien.

Eisenmann. *Dix Ans d'Histoire Constitutionelle d'Autrichienne, 1918–28.* Paris. M. Giard, 1928.

Froelich, Georg. *Österreichisches Staatsrecht.* Die Handelshochschule Lieferung. 92. Ausgabe B.

Froelich u. Adamovich. *Die österreichischen Verfassungsgesetze.* January 1930.

Graham, M. W. *New Governments of Central Europe.* Holt, New York; Pitman, London. 1924.

'The Constitutional Crisis in Austria,' *American Political Science Review*, vol. xxiv, 1932.

Headlam-Morley, Agnes. *The New Democratic Constitutions of Europe.* Oxford University Press, 1928.

**Jahrbuch des Offentlichen Rechts.* Tübingen. Vols ix, xi, xv, xviii.

Kelsen, Hans. *Österreichisches Staatsrecht.* Tübingen, Mohr. 1923.

Merkl, Adolf. '*Der rechtliche Gehalt der österreichischen Verfassungsreform vom 7 Dezember 1929*', *Zeitschrift für öffentliches Recht:* Vol. x, heft 2. Wien.

'Die Verwaltungsgesetzebung der österreichischen Republik', *Jahrbuch des öffentlichen Rechts.* Vol. xv.

Seipel, Ignaz. *Der Kampf um die österreichische Verfassung.* Wien u. Leipzig, 1930.

Gedanken zur österreichischen Verfassungsreform. Innsbruck, 1917.

**Stenographische Verhandlungsschrift über die Länderkonferenz in Salzburg, am 15, 16, 17 Februar 1920.* Verlag der Landesregierung in Salsburg.

**Stenographische Verhandlungsschrift über die Länderkonferenz in Linz, am 20, 21, 22, 23 April 1930.* Verlag des Oberösterreichischen Landesrates in Linz.

Verdier, Abel. *La Constitution fédérale de la Republique d'Autriche.* Thèse pour le Doctorat, Paris, 1924.

Zurcher, A. J. *The Experiment with Democracy in Central Europe.* Oxford University Press, London and New York, 1932.

III. Political History

Alarmruf aus Österreich. Ein Blick hinter die Kulissen der Reaktion. Frankfurt, 1931. Von einem österreichischen Beamten.

*Bauer, Otto. *The Austrian Revolution.* Translated by H. J. Stenning. Parsons, London, 1925.

Sozialdemokratie, Religion u. Kirche. Wien, 1927.

Der Aufstand der Massen. Prague, 1934.

Borkenau, Franz. *Austria and After.* Faber and Faber, London, 1938.

Braunthal, Julius. *Die Wiener Julitage*, 1927.

Brockhausen, Karl. *Die politische Struktur des heutigen Österreich.* Sonderabdruck aus Zeitschrift für die gesamte Staatswissenschaft, 80. Jahrgang. 1925. Verlag der H. Laupp'schen. Buchhandlung in Tübingen.

Germains, V. W. *Austria of To-day.* Macmillan, London, 1932.

Hakenkreuz gegen Österreich. Das Braunbuch. Wien. Bundeskanzleramt. Österreichische Staatsdruckerei, 1933.

Hemala, Dr. F. *Christliche oder Freie Gewerkschaften?* Verlag der typographischen Anstalt. Wien.

Jászi, Oscar. *The Dissolution of the Habsburg Monarchy.* University of Chicago Press, 1929.

*Knoll (ed.) *Kardinal Piffl u. der österreichische Episkopat zu sozialen u. kulturellen Fragen, 1913–32.* Reinhold Verlag, Wien, 1932.

Knoll, A. M. *Von Seipel zu Dollfuss.* 1934.

Kunschak, Leopold. *Österreich, 1918–34.* 2 Auflage. Wien, 1935. (Typographische Anstalt, Wien.)

Lux, P. T. *La Leçon de l'Autriche, 1919–37.* Attinger, Paris, 1937.

Macartney, C. A. *The Social Revolution in Austria.* Cambridge University Press, London, 1926.

'Austria since 1928', *Slavonic Review*, vol. viii, 1928–9.

'The Armed Formations of Austria,' *Journal of the Institute of International Affairs*, vol. viii, 1929.

Hungary and Her Successors: The Treaty of Trianon and its Consequences. Oxford University Press for Royal Institute of International Affairs, 1937.

Messner, Johannes. *Dollfuss, an Austrian Patriot.* Burns, Oates, London, 1935.
Die Soziale Frage. 2nd edition. Verlagsanstalt Tyrolia. 1938.
Millin, S. G. *General Smuts.* 2 vols. Faber and Faber, London, 1936.
Nowak. *Collapse of Central Europe.* (Trans. P. Lochner and E. W. Dickes.) Kegan Paul, London, 1924.
Redlich, Joseph. *The Emperor Francis Joseph of Austria.* Macmillan, London, 1929.
Austrian War Government. Yale University Press, New Haven, 1929.
Riehl, Dr. Walter. *Geschichte des Nationalsozialismus in Österreich.* Forum Verlag. Leipzig, 1933.
Schuschnigg, Kurt von. *Farewell, Austria.* Cassell, London, 1938.
Seipel, Ignaz. *Nation u. Staat.* Wien u. Leipzig, 1916.
**Social Democratic Party Conference Reports.*
Trevelyan, G. M. *Grey of Fallodon.* Longmans, London, 1937.
von Glaise-Horstenau, Edmund. *The Collapse of the Austro-Hungarian Empire.* (Trans. F. D. Morrow.) Dent, London and Toronto, 1930.

IV. Foreign Policy

Ball, Margaret M. *Post-war German-Austrian Relations, 1918-36.* Stanford University Press, California, and Oxford University Press, London, 1931.
Beneš, Eduard. 'The Austro-German Customs House Project', *Czechoslovak Sources and Documents.* Orbis, Prague, 1931.
Speech delivered in the Chamber of Deputies, Prague, 23 April 1931. *Czechoslovak Sources and Documents.* Orbis, Prague.
Bitterman, M., 'Austria and the Customs Union', *Czechoslovak Sources and Documents.* Orbis, Prague, 1931.
British Year Book of International Law. 'The Austro-German

Customs Union Case.' Oxford University Press, London, 1932.

Currey, Muriel. *Italian Foreign Policy, 1918–32*. Ivor Nicolson and Watson, London, 1932.

Kleinwaechter, Friedrich F. G. *Selbstbestimmungsrecht für Österreich*. Stuttgart. Deutsche Verlags-Anstalt. 1929.

Kleinwaechter, Friedrich F. G., Paller, Heinz von (editors). *Die Anschlussfrage in ihrer kulturellen, politischen, u. wirtschaftlichen Bedeutung*. Wien, Leipzig. Wm. Braumüller, 1930.

League of Nations. *Austrian Protocol*. Geneva, 15 July 1932. C. 539, 270. 1932, II, A.

Commission of Inquiry for European Union. Minutes. 1930–1. VII.

Documents relating to the Organization of a System of European Federal Union. Geneva. 15 September 1930. A. 46, 1930. VII.

Macartney, H. H. M., and Cremona, P. *Italy's Foreign and Colonial Policy, 1914–37*.

Permanent Court of International Justice. Series C. Pleadings, Oral Statements and Documents, XXII Session, 1931. No. 53, 'Customs régime between Germany and Austria.' Series A-B, Judgements, Orders and Advisory Opinions, No. 41. 'Customs régime between Germany and Austria.'

V. Economic Questions

Argus. *The Economic Aspects of the Austro-German Customs Union*. Orbis, Prague, 1931.

Great Britain. Department of Overseas Trade Reports.

*Hainisch, Michael. *Die Landflucht*. Jena, 1924.

League of Nations. *Ten Years of World Co-operation*. 1932.

Economic and Financial. 1932, E.781.

Etudes relatives au problème des rapprochements européennes. Chiffres essentiels du commerce exterieur des pays danubiens.

The Economic Situation of Austria. Report presented to the Council of the League of Nations by W. T. Layton,

C. H. and Charles Rist. Geneva, 19 August 1925. C. 440 (I), 162. 1925 (II).

The Financial Reconstruction of Austria, 1926. Geneva, November 1926. C. 568, M. 232, 1926, II.

The Restoration of Austria. Agreements arranged by the League of Nations, and signed at Geneva on 4 October 1922, with the relevant Documents and Public Statements. C. 716, M. 428, 1922, X. Geneva, 1922.

Pasvolsky. *Economic Nationalism of the States.* Allen and Unwin, London, 1928.

Only books which are of particular value, either by reason of their authorship or their contents, have been included in this list.

The following newspapers and periodicals have been used. Those of particular value are indicated by an asterisk.

**Arbeiter Zeitung.*
Daily Telegraph.
Frankfurter Zeitung.
**Kampf.*
Le Temps.
Manchester Guardian.
**Neue Freie Presse.*
Neues Wiener Journal.
Neues Wiener Tageblatt.
Pester Lloyd.
Prager Presse.
**Reichspost.*
The Times.

INDEX

PRINTED IN GREAT BRITAIN
BY WESTERN PRINTING SERVICES LTD., BRISTOL